JUST TACOS

100 Delicious Recipes for Breakfast, Lunch, and Dinner

SHELLEY WISEMAN

PHOTOGRAPHY BY ROMULO YANES

The Taunton Press

To Liam, Louis, Lucas, Olive, Mitchel, Felix, Vita, Niels, and Bas, my nieces and nephews who bring joy to my life.

The Taunton Press
Inspiration for hands-on living®

The Taunton Press, Inc., 63 South Main Street
PO Box 5506, Newtown, CT 06470-5506
e-mail: tp@taunton.com

Editor: Carolyn Mandarano
Copy Editor: Nina Rynd Whitman
Indexer: Jay Kreider
Cover design: Teresa Fernandes
Interior design: Carol Singer
Layout: Amy Griffin
Photographer: Romulo Yanes
Food Stylist: Paul Grimes
Prop Stylist: Philippa Brathwaite

The following names/manufacturers appearing in Just Tacos are trademarks:
Abuelita®, Breville®, Coca-Cola®, Goya®, Maggi®, Maseca®, Oster®, Play-Doh®, Tabasco®

Library of Congress Cataloging-in-Publication Data
Wiseman, Shelton, 1956-
 Just tacos : 100 delicious recipes for breakfast, lunch, and dinner / Shelley
Wiseman ; photographer, Romulo Yanes.
    p. cm.
 Includes index.
 ISBN 978-1-60085-407-1
 1. Tacos. 2. Cookbooks. I. Title.
 TX836.W57 2011
 641.84--dc23
                    2011029268

Printed in the United States of America
10 9 8 7 6 5 4 3 2 1

Acknowledgments

First and foremost I would like to thank my friend and mentor, Roberto Santibañez, for being so generous with his knowledge and spirit. I would also like to thank other Mexican chefs who have inspired me: Maria Dolores Torres Yzábal, an extraordinary woman and my former co-author; Diana Kennedy, who first brought real Mexican cuisine to this country and created a high standard; Ricardo Muñoz Zurita, for his exquisite palate and huge historical food knowledge; Federico Rigoletti, for sharing his time and expertise with me and for the finesse of his sensibility with seafood; and the lively Roberto Craig and the quirky David Ortega for sharing their recipes.

I would like to thank Taunton Press for giving me the opportunity to write this book; my editor, Carolyn Mandarano, for her guidance; and my agent, Doe Coover, for her always-available helping hand.

The quality of this book is greatly enhanced by the photography of my former *Gourmet* magazine colleague, Romulo Yanes, and the acute artistic eye of food stylist Paul Grimes.

I would like to thank all my neighbors for being willing tasters (and dish washers), notably Raychel O'Shea Patiño, James Viskochil, Nicky Lee, and Mark Tyner.

I would like to thank my family and friends for keeping me sane, as the act of writing a book can get lonely.

Finally, I would like to thank my assistant, Rebecca Rosas, for her hard work and companionship.

Contents

Introduction

⇥ Tacos, that humble Mexican street food, have entered the popular food culture to such an extent in the U.S. (and increasingly around the world) that other cuisines, notably Korean, are discovering them as a way to sell their own cultural dishes. Even high-end restaurants of other cultural orientations, like Nobu, the Japanese-Peruvian restaurant empire, are including tacos on their menu.

Why are tacos so popular?

In an increasingly fast-paced world, a taco is the quintessential food on the go. Essentially anything can be enclosed in a tortilla—add an interesting sauce, some crunchy onions, and you're good to go. In fact, the best tacos are eaten as soon as they are made. Like pancakes, you serve one person at a time directly from the stove, which is why taco trucks are so popular.

While eating tacos and other Mexican foods has become part of our everyday life, cooking Mexican food has not yet. That is where this book comes in. Here I have included many fillings that are easy to make for a simple and satisfying meal, whether it is a steak freshly sliced from the grill or a roast chicken tossed with onion and topped with a good salsa. There are many options for vegetarians, from straight refried beans with crumbled cheese to the more exotic grilled nopal cactus pads with fresh tomato salsa. I've also included some dishes that are a bit more involved, though not overly difficult. Some of these are dishes that could be served on their own as well as serve as a taco filling and often can be frozen. So if you have time to prepare in advance, you can still put a meal, even a feast for many, together quickly.

It is the fun of eating tacos that attracts people—messy, satisfying stand-up food lends itself to casual gatherings and easy conversations. A few margaritas don't go amiss either, and I have included an unusual tequila drink made with pineapple to add to your repertoire.

I have concentrated on classic Mexican tacos, some with strong regional identities and many from the cosmopolitan melting pot of Mexico City, where I lived for many years. I also have added some modern variations from local chefs and of my own creation. What I have stayed clear of are the commercial hard-shelled tacos that seem to have been invented by the U.S. food industry a generation ago and can still be found in national food chains. Newer chains, while using soft tortillas, still overload the chosen (but often insipid) meat with so much beans, guacamole, and shredded lettuce that you can't taste the meat anymore.

Varieties of tacos

Perhaps the most famous, but fairly modern, taco invented in Mexico City is the *taco al pastor*, with its layers of adobo-marinated pork (or chicken) roasted on a vertical spit to mimic the Middle Eastern lamb spit (Mexico City has a large Lebanese population). Tacos focusing on grilled meats are called *tacos al carbon*, which often have as accompaniments grilled spring onions or roasted serrano chiles. In many Mexican marketplaces you will find taco stands focusing on quesadillas, which are made starting with raw tortilla dough and filled before the tortilla is fully cooked. This is where you will find a great variety of vegetable fillings that also work for tacos: cooked mushrooms, nopales, swiss chard, potatoes, and, of course, cheese.

The largest variety of tacos are *tacos de guisados*. A *guisado* is simply a cooked dish. These are homestyle preparations in great *cazuelas* (Mexican casserole dishes) that are brought from a home kitchen to a stand and served up to order. These might include chiles rellenos, pork adobo, or even mole poblano. *Tacos de carnitas* are in a class of their own and are found in specialized places. *Carnitas* are made by cooking large hunks of pork in water and enough pork fat to brown the meat once the water has cooked them.

Fish tacos are mostly from the extensive coastlines of Mexico (although lake regions have their own specialties, like *charrales*, tiny fried fish tacos). Those found in the Baja peninsula are very different from those found in Veracruz, while Puerto Vallarta seems to have a corner on the smoked marlin market.

The tacos included in this book are just a beginning, as the subject is inexhaustible. I hope you will enjoy these as well as create some of your own.

Salsas

Salsas are another vast subject and should not be thought of solely for their heat. Adding heat is definitely one of their jobs, but we could simply have a bottle of Tabasco® on the table if that was the end of it. Compare the fruity heat of a mango and habanero salsa with the sharp acidity of a raw tomatillo salsa or serrano-lime salsa; the smoky heat of a chipotle salsa with the mild herbaceous heat of a poblano sauce. For grilled meats, salsas also supply a juicy dimension, and the appropriate salsas are quite liquid (cooked tomatillo salsa) or have juicy elements like tomatoes. There is nothing to stop you from using more than one salsa at a time either, as a typical taco stand will have at least two, usually a red and a green to choose from.

Have a taco party!

If you have a backyard, you can get a large comal (or large pizza pan) to go over a candy burner and have an eat-as-you-go or make-your-own taco party complete with a bar of fillings, salsas, and fixings.

If you like to grill, consider the Grilled Garlic-Marinated Skirt Steak with Charred Spring Onions (pp. 121-122), Grilled Shrimp in Adobo (p. 63), and Grilled Cactus Pads (p. 44).

If you prefer make-ahead fillings that can be reheated on

the stove or in the oven, choose from any of the braised fillings. A well-rounded selection includes Pork in Green Sauce (p. 95), Duck Legs Braised in Chipotle-Tomatillo Sauce (p. 87), Swiss Chard and Potato (p. 29), and tender Octopus with Pickled Jalapeños, Olives, and Capers (p. 67).

Some fillings, such as Lobster and Mango Salsa (p. 65), Chopped Fish and Tomatillo "Salad" (p. 56), and, of course, Guacamole (p. 34), work well at room temperature, so all you need at the last minute are hot tortillas. This could make a quick-to-put-together taco lunch party.

For kids, I have had great success with a choose-your-own-filling quesadilla party, using store-bought tortillas and offering a choice of shredded cheese, simple refried beans, sautéed mushrooms, and chicken with onions to mix and match. The idea is that when you heat the second side of the tortilla you add the chosen fillings, then you fold the tortilla and heat it some more on each side to melt the cheese and heat the fillings, then deliver it on a plate. Have guacamole and salsa (with only a touch of chile, if at all) on the side to add. Be sure to treat the kids to a fruit cooler (p. 143) to wash it down with!

Another kid-friendly choice, since all kids like fried food, is the Baja Fish Tacos (p. 53). Just be sure to seed the chipotle chiles before adding them to the mayonnaise accompaniment and add a little at a time to taste, or just make a lime mayonnaise and mix it with the shredded cabbage like a slaw.

I've tried to give you a large selection of tacos to choose from for any occasion, but sometimes it is hard to know where to start. I hope these suggestions will help. Enjoy!

Tortillas

The last 30 years have seen a huge explosion of Mexican food in the U.S., especially tortillas and tortilla chips. You can buy these packaged goods just about everywhere. But even though these are readily available, their taste doesn't compare to that of freshly made corn or flour tortillas. Although making your own tortillas can seem a bit daunting, it's actually quite fun.

I have included recipes for making corn and flour tortillas from scratch. While I have given you the simple method of making corn tortillas from widely available corn tortilla flour (masa harina), I have also taken a leap of faith and given you a recipe starting from corn kernels and using your food processor. I say a leap of faith because it is not easy to find the regular white or blue corn kernels used in Mexico. Tortilleria Nixtamal in Queens, New York, the only tortilla producer in the state to use corn instead of masa harina, gets its corn from a wholesale producer in Indiana specifically geared to the

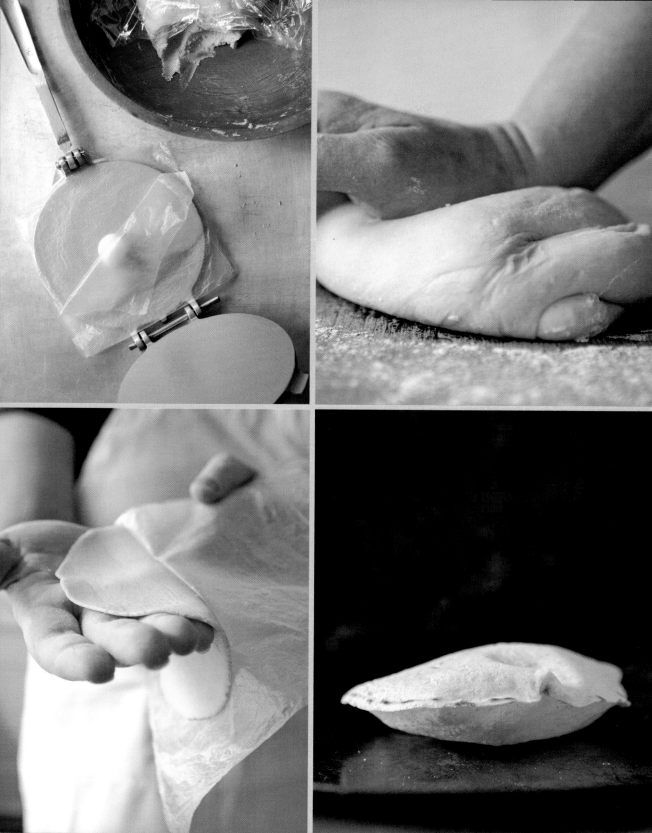

tortilla market. Occasionally, though, you will see a bin of corn kernels in a neighborhood Mexican market. If you do, buy some along with some cal (see the sidebar on p. 18) to make your own. I have created my recipe around the pozole corn kernels I see in regular supermarkets, which work, even though they are already peeled, so they don't have tough skins to remove.

Flavored tortillas are becoming increasingly popular—I saw several flavors of flour tortillas for sale on my last trip to Mexico—and you may soon see them in U.S. markets. Here you'll find three flavor variations on corn tortillas—adobo (dried chile based), black bean, and hibiscus—and one for flour tortillas—cilantro. Since the trick is adding the flavor to the water used in the recipe you could experiment further if you wish.

While corn tortillas are pressed (see the sidebar on p. 12 for information on tortilla presses), flour tortillas need to be rolled out like pastry dough because of the gluten in the wheat flour. There are small rolling pins made for the task, but a cut dowel or a regular rolling pin works perfectly fine as well. Find out how to knead and roll out the dough on p. 21.

Corn Tortillas from Tortilla Flour

Tortillas de maiz de masa harina

**MAKES 1¼ POUNDS DOUGH;
ABOUT FOURTEEN 5½- TO
6-INCH TORTILLAS, THIRTY
TO FORTY 4-INCH TORTILLAS,
AND FIFTY TO SIXTY 3-INCH
HORS D'OEUVRE TORTILLAS**

2 cups corn tortilla flour
(masa harina, such as
Maseca®)

½ teaspoon salt

1½ to 1¾ cups warm water

EQUIPMENT
A tortilla press and two
6-inch rounds of plastic cut
from thin grocery bags or
zip-top bags

The trick to making tortillas is to get a rhythm going so that you can make more than one at a time, though at the beginning you may want to go slowly so you can time what you are doing. It is a good idea to get a comal, a griddle that is about 12 inches wide, or buy a long double griddle that will fit over two burners. The tortillas should puff when they have been turned over twice, a satisfying sight and a sign that they are about done and ready to be kept warm in a cloth-lined tortilla basket.

MAKE THE DOUGH

Combine the tortilla flour, salt, and 1½ cups water in a large bowl and knead with your hands until a uniform dough forms, 1 to 2 minutes. The dough should be slightly moister than fresh Play-Doh® but just stiff enough to form into a ball. If necessary, knead a little more water into the dough. Let stand, covered with plastic wrap, for 5 minutes. The dough will dry out as it sits, so keep it covered with plastic wrap as you work.

For 5½- to 6-inch tortillas: Pinch off 1½ ounces of dough and form into a 1½-inch ball. Form more balls as you press and cook them.

For 4-inch tortillas: Pinch off ½ ounce dough and form a ¾-inch ball. Form more balls as you press and cook them.

For 3-inch mini-tortillas: Pinch off ⅓ ounce dough and form into a scant ¾-inch ball. Form more balls as you press and cook them.

FLATTEN AND COOK THE TORTILLAS

Heat a flat griddle over medium heat until hot, about 2 minutes.

Press the ball of dough between the plastic rounds in the tortilla press to form the tortilla. If at all uneven, rotate the tortilla 180 degrees and press again to the desired size. Peel off 1 plastic round, then, holding the tortilla over the edge of your palm, care-

Making Corn Tortillas

Put a small ball of dough between plastic squares or circles (cut from plastic grocery bags or thin plastic storage bags) in the tortilla press.

Flatten the corn tortilla and remove the top piece of plastic

Drape about one third of the tortilla over the side of your palm and remove the second piece of plastic.

Gently lay the tortilla on the griddle, moving your hand backwards and turning your palm to release the tortilla as you do so.

If all goes well, your tortilla will puff up when it has been flipped twice and is finishing cooking. If it doesn't, that's OK too!

fully peel off the other round so the tortilla is dangling from your palm. Transfer the tortilla to the griddle by letting the dangling edge touch it and slowly pulling your hand back as you lay the tortilla down on the griddle. This will take a little practice, but it is better than flipping the tortillas onto the griddle because they rarely end up lying flat.

Cook until the edges lift just slightly from the griddle, about 15 seconds. Turn over (you can lift the edge of the tortilla with a butter knife or spatula to help you but then grab it with your fingers and flip it over). Cook until a few faint brown spots appear on the underside, about 45 seconds. Turn over again and cook until the tortilla inflates slightly (this may not always happen) and small brown spots appear on the second side, 30 to 45 seconds. Transfer the tortilla to a cloth-lined tortilla basket to keep warm as you make more tortillas.

NOTE: *Cooked tortillas should be eaten while they are still warm, but they can be reheated on the griddle or in the oven up to a couple of hours after making. The dough will last chilled in a tightly sealed plastic bag for 1 day.*

Equipment for Perfect Tortillas

TORTILLA PRESSES

→ The most common tortilla press is made from cast metal, and the best of those is made by Estrella, and is available from www.thelatinproducts .com (or by calling 800-694-8344). It is easy to find cheap cast-iron or cast-aluminum ones in stores in Latino neighborhoods, but they are just that—cheap. They may work, but you run the risk of the disks being uneven and having imperfections. There are also wooden versions that are square rather than round. The Latino Products company sells two, a larger pine version good for making tortillas larger than 6 inches and a smaller one that's finished mesquite (which may need a little sanding).

PLASTIC FOR LINING THE DISKS

Crucial to making tortillas are the pieces of plastic to line the disks. You need to cut out 2 rounds or squares about an inch larger than the tortillas you want to make. The perfect thickness is that of plastic grocery bags, which are about halfway between plastic wrap and zip-top bags. If you are using zip-top bags, use thinner ones. You can cut the sides and locking end of the bags and leave the two sides in one piece, though I think it is easier to have two separate round or square pieces. These can be wiped off and reused over and over again, so store them inside your press.

COMAL

In Mexico there are two main types of comals (from the Nahuatl for flat pan, *comalli*), which are flat cooking surfaces used mainly for cooking tortillas, though also for dry-roasting or toasting anything from tomatoes to dried chiles.

The first type is an unglazed ceramic disk anywhere from 10 to 30 inches in diameter that has a gentle curve up to the edges. It is used largely in areas like Oaxaca and the valley of Cuautla in Morelos, or anywhere a lot of ceramics are made. It is very fragile so you probably won't see them sold anywhere in the U.S. A ceramic comal needs to be cured with a mixture of cal (calcium hydroxide; see p. 18) and water to make the surface less porous, a sort of ancient nonstick pan.

The second type of comal is a flat disk of some kind of metal. The large ones in the markets (up to about 3 feet or more across) are sometimes cut from a metal oil drum.

The ones you can buy usually have a handle to hang them up by and a very small, often sloped lip for stability. Some are cast iron, but most are a thinner sheet metal. You'll need to apply a thin coating of oil the first time you use this type of comal, but that's all you need to get started. It is best to wipe the comal clean between uses rather than wash it, as it can rust. For this reason I prefer not to roast tomatoes or tomatillos on a comal but rather to use a broiler or a toaster oven.

In the recipes I have simply called for a flat griddle, and I've used everything from a pizza pan (it will warp but it works really well, and I like something big enough so I can move cooked items away from the center heat, which is especially true when making hors d'oeuvres with toppings) to a nonstick Indian dosa pan, my current favorite. Many stoves come with a griddle built in, which works very well, or you can use a two-burner griddle. I avoid using a skillet because it is easy to burn your hands on the sides.

When flipping the tortillas over, good Mexican cooks will just use their fingers, but it can help to have a small spatula just to lift the edge so the tortillas are easy to grab.

BLENDER

A good blender is indispensable for Mexican cooking. It is used for everything from blending salsas to moles as well as making the wonderful simple fruit drinks *aguas frescas*. A blender is not interchangeable with a food processor, which will not grind the chiles or spices finely enough. A food processor doesn't work very well for primarily liquid mixtures, since they tend to fly out of the seal and make a mess of the kitchen.

What to look for in a blender? Often the cheaper ones are just fine and tend to have the preferred shape of the tapered sides. If you are buying a blender with wide, straight sides, look for one that has a concave or flat bottom with wide blades, such as a Breville®. Those that have a gulley with small blades are problematic for grinding the spices in Mexican sauces. Look for a strong motor and a glass jar—you'll be grinding many sauces continuously for up to 3 minutes. Another good choice is the metal-based Oster®, the classic bartender's blender with a toggle switch. What you don't need are lots of speeds.

Black-Bean-Flavored Corn Tortillas

Tortillas de maiz con sabor de frijol

MAKES ABOUT 1½ POUNDS DOUGH; ABOUT FORTY 4-INCH TORTILLAS

½ cup cooked black beans

½ teaspoon salt

1½ to 1¾ cups warm bean cooking liquid or water

2 cups corn tortilla flour (masa harina, such as Maseca)

EQUIPMENT

A tortilla press and two 6-inch rounds of plastic cut from thin grocery bags or plastic zip-top bags

I like making small (4-inch) tortillas with this dough as they are quite delicate and absolutely delicious, especially if you are making them with the broth from homemade beans.

→ Put the beans, salt, and 1½ cups cooking liquid or water in a blender and blend until smooth, about 1 minute. Put the tortilla flour in a bowl and add the blended mixture. Knead with your hands as for regular tortillas. The dough should be moist like soft Play-Doh. Add a little more water if necessary to get the right consistency. Let stand, covered with plastic wrap, for 5 minutes. The dough will dry out as it sits, so keep it covered with plastic wrap as you work.

Make ½-ounce (¾-inch) balls for 4-inch tortillas and follow the directions for making tortillas on pp. 9–11.

NOTE: *The tortillas are best eaten right away, but they can be reheated on the griddle or in the oven up to a couple of hours after making. Chill any leftover tortillas in a tightly sealed plastic bag for making tortilla chips (totopos) up to a day later.*

Chile-Flavored Corn Tortillas

Tortillas de maiz con adobo

MAKES 1¼ POUNDS DOUGH; ABOUT FOURTEEN 5- TO 6-INCH TORTILLAS, THIRTY TO FORTY 4-INCH TORTILLAS, AND FIFTY TO SIXTY 3-INCH HORS D'OEUVRE TORTILLAS

1⅓ cups warm water

⅓ cup Adobo Marinade (p. 128)

2 cups corn tortilla flour (masa harina, such as Maseca)

½ teaspoon salt

EQUIPMENT
A tortilla press and two 5-inch rounds of plastic cut from thin grocery bags or plastic zip-top bags

These reddish tortillas have an earthy flavor that I like with some of the vegetable and breakfast tacos because they contrast with the filling. They're also great with a dried chile- or adobo-flavored filling.

➡ Stir together the water and the Adobo Marinade. In a bowl, combine the tortilla flour with the salt, and stir in the water and adobo mixture; knead until a smooth dough forms, about 1 minute. The dough should be moist like soft Play-Doh. Add a little more water or tortilla flour if necessary to get the right consistency. Let stand, covered with plastic wrap, for 5 minutes. The dough will dry out as it sits, so keep it covered with plastic wrap as you work.

Make 1½-ounce (¾-inch) balls for 5½-inch tortillas and follow the directions for making tortillas on pp. 9–11.

NOTE: *The tortillas are best eaten right away, but they can be reheated on the griddle or in the oven up to a couple of hours after making. Chill any leftover tortillas in a tightly sealed plastic bag for making tortilla chips* (totopos) *up to a day later.*

Hibiscus-Flavored Corn Tortillas

Tortillas de maiz con flor de Jamaica

MAKES 1¼ POUNDS DOUGH; ABOUT FOURTEEN 5- TO 6-INCH TORTILLAS, THIRTY TO FORTY 4-INCH TORTILLAS, AND FIFTY TO SIXTY 3-INCH HORS D'OEUVRE TORTILLAS

1½ to 1¾ cups warm Hibiscus Cooler (p. 86)

½ teaspoon salt

2 cups corn tortilla flour (masa harina, such as Maseca)

EQUIPMENT

A tortilla press and two 5-inch rounds of plastic cut from thin grocery bags or plastic zip-top bags

These make such bright magenta-colored tortillas that you might think they're made from beets. The flavor is slightly reminiscent of earthy sour dough, and they're excellent with mushrooms or *huitlacoche*, corn mushrooms (see p. 30).

Stir together the Hibiscus Cooler, salt, and tortilla flour in a bowl and knead until a smooth dough forms, about 1 minute. The dough should be moist like soft Play-Doh. Add a little more water or tortilla flour if necessary to get the right consistency.

Follow the directions for making tortillas on pp. 9–11.

NOTE: *The tortillas are best eaten right away, but they can be reheated on the griddle or in the oven up to a couple of hours after making. Chill any leftover tortillas in a tightly sealed plastic bag for making tortilla chips* (totopos) *up to a day later.*

MEXICAN PANTRY

Hibiscus Flowers

The flavor of dried hibiscus flowers *(flor de Jamaica)* is rich and fruity with a light acidity. The flowers are sold loose or in bags in Mexican supermarkets and can be ordered online from Amazon.com.

Corn Tortilla Dough from Scratch

Masa para tortillas

**MAKES 3¾ POUNDS MASA;
ABOUT FORTY 5- TO 6-INCH
TORTILLAS**

3 quarts water for cooking
the corn

2 lb. dried corn kernel or
2 (14-ounce) packages dry
hominy corn kernels (such as
Goya brand; a scant 6 cups)

2 tablespoons cal (powdered
limestone; calcium hydroxide),
diluted in 1 cup cold water

About 1⅓ cups water for
processing the masa

1½ teaspoons salt

As an alternative to using dried tortilla flour (masa harina) to make corn tortillas, you can start with dried corn kernels. The process of boiling and soaking the corn with processed powdered limestone (cal) is called *nixtamalizado*, and it softens the corn so the skins can be removed and the kernels can be ground. While this process also releases some of the corn's nutrients (in particular niacin, so it can be absorbed by the body), it also is what gives tortillas their unique flavor.

Hominy is a good substitution for dried corn because it is widely available in supermarkets in the U.S. Hominy are large white kernels and are usually sold *pelado,* or peeled, so the step of rubbing the skins off is not necessary. Brands such as Goya® are labeled "giant white corn/maiz mote pelado." If you have a Mexican grocer near you, look for regular dried white or blue corn kernels (don't use popcorn kernels!). Or order blue corn pozole (and cal) from www.latinmerchant.com.

Bring the 3 quarts water to a boil in a 5- to 6-quart pot. Add the corn and bring back to a boil. Restir the cal in the cup of water (it will turn milky), then stir into the pot (the corn will turn yellow). Turn the heat down and cook, without boiling, stirring occasionally, until some of skin rubs off a kernel (if using regular dried corn) when rubbed hard between your fingers, about 5 minutes.

Turn off the heat and let the corn soak at room temperature for at least 8 hours and up to 24.

Rub the corn kernels against each other in the pot with your hands, grabbing a handful at a time to rub off skins (which will now rub off easily; omit this step if using peeled corn), then rinse in several changes of cold water to remove the skin residue and the cal. Drain the corn.

Working in batches of 2 cups of corn and ¼ to ⅓ cup water, process the corn in a food processor, pulsing about 20 times, then puréeing for about 5 minutes, scraping down the sides occasionally, or until the masa no longer feels gritty.

Transfer each batch of masa (you will have about 4 batches) to a wide bowl as they're processed. Mix in the salt with your hands.

Make tortillas as described in Corn Tortillas from Tortilla Flour on pp. 9–11.

NOTE: *The tortilla dough will keep chilled in a sealed plastic bag for 2 days.*

What Is Cal?

Cal, a white powder that is made from limestone, is essential to nixtamalnation, the process for preparing corn. Chemically, food-grade cal is calcium hydroxide. Joe Ebeling of Mississippi Lime, a limestone quarry in Illinois, explained the process to me: Small chunks of limestone (calcium carbonate, chemically $CaCO_3$) are heated to red hot (around 2,000°F) so that the carbon dioxide (CO_2) is released into the air, leaving behind about half the original volume of calcium oxide, or quick lime (CaO), which is very unstable. The quick lime is then mixed with just enough water (H_2O) to make a still-powdered mixture called calcium hydroxide $Ca(OH)_2$. The powder goes through a variety of sieves. Coarser grades are used for construction while the finest grade is used for food.

Food-grade cal can sometimes be found in small packages in the Latino section of some supermarkets and can be ordered from www.latinmerchant.com or www.mrswagesstore.com, where it is sold as "pickling lime" in 16-ounce packages.

Flour Tortillas

Tortillas de harina

**MAKES 1 POUND DOUGH;
TWELVE 6-INCH TORTILLAS
OR FOUR 10-INCH TORTILLAS**

2¼ cups all-purpose flour

1 teaspoon salt

¼ cup pork lard, cut into pieces

1 tablespoon vegetable oil

¾ cup warm water

Flour tortillas are from northern Mexico, where a wheat culture replaces the corn culture of the center and south. I have suggested using them with some of the typical meat dishes from the north as well as with some delicate seafood preparations whose flavor is easily overwhelmed by the more assertive flavor of the corn tortillas. In general, though, let your personal taste guide you.

➡️ Stir together the flour and the salt in a large bowl. Add the pork lard and blend with your fingers (as for pastry dough) until the mixture resembles fine meal. Drizzle the vegetable oil over the mixture and stir in the warm water with a fork until a dough forms. Knead the dough on a work surface until it is soft and elastic, about 5 minutes.

Let the dough stand in a bowl covered with plastic wrap for 1 hour.

Roll the dough into a 10- to 12-inch sausage and divide into 12 pieces.

Heat a flat griddle over medium heat until hot, about 2 minutes.

Turn a piece of dough in a little flour and, using as little extra flour as possible (you don't want flour residue on the outside of the tortillas), roll out with a rolling pin or a 7-inch dowel. Once a small round form, roll from below the center out in one direction, turning the dough about an eighth of a turn at a time and rolling out again until you have a very thin 6-inch round. Brush off any visible flour from both sides of the tortilla.

Put the tortilla on the griddle and cook until pale brown spots appear on the underside, about 45 seconds. Turn over (you can lift the edge of the tortilla with a butter knife or spatula to help you but then grab it with your fingers and flip it over). Cook on the second side until pale brown spots appear, about 45 seconds more. (The tortillas should stay supple; if you cook the tortillas too long they will stiffen.) Transfer the tortilla to a cloth-lined tortilla basket to keep warm. Make more tortillas in the same manner.

For large (10-inch) tortillas: Roll the dough into a thick 8-inch log and cut into four pieces. Roll out into 10-inch rounds following the directions on p. 19. If you have difficulty keeping the dough round, roll it slightly larger and cut out a round using a 10-inch plate as a guide.

NOTE: *The tortillas are best eaten freshly made. If necessary, reheat them on the griddle for 15 seconds a side or wrap them 6 to 8 at a time in foil and heat in a 350°F oven for 8 to 10 minutes. Leftover tortillas can be made into chips (see p. 23).*

VARIATION

You can make the tortillas without the pork lard. Use 5 tablespoons vegetable oil and drizzle it over the flour mixture. Stir with a fork to coat beads of oil with flour, then blend with your fingers until the mixture resembles fine meal and add the water. Continue as above.

Kneading and Cooking Flour Tortilla Dough

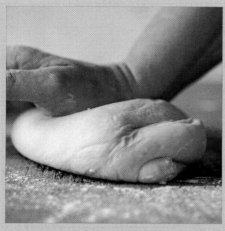

Knead the flour tortilla dough until it's soft and smooth.

Roll out a piece of the flour tortilla dough to a paper-thin 6-inch flour tortilla.

Turn the tortilla over once small brown spots appear on the underside, about 45 seconds, then cook for another 45 seconds on the second side.

Cilantro-Flavored Flour Tortillas

Tortillas de harina con cilantro

MAKES TWELVE 6-INCH TORTILLAS OR FOUR 10-INCH TORTILLAS

6 cups water

1 small bunch cilantro (4 ounces)

1 teaspoon salt

2¼ cups all-purpose flour

¼ cup pork lard, cut into pieces

1 tablespoon vegetable oil

The herb flavor of these tortillas works well with seafood, beans, and vegetable tacos as well as breakfast tacos.

Bring the water to a boil in a 3-quart saucepan. Cut the top 6 inches from the cilantro (include the tender stems), add to the boiling water, and cook for 1 minute. Reserve ¾ cup of the cooking water, then drain the cilantro in a sieve and transfer the cilantro and the reserved water to a blender along with the salt; blend until smooth. Transfer to a measuring cup and let cool.

Put the flour in a large bowl. Add the pork lard and blend with your fingers (as for pastry dough) until the mixture resembles fine meal. Drizzle the vegetable oil over the mixture and stir in ¾ cup of the cilantro water with a fork until a dough forms. Knead the dough on a work surface until it's soft and elastic, about 5 minutes.

Let the dough stand in a bowl covered with plastic wrap for 1 hour.

Follow the instructions for making tortillas in Flour Tortillas on pp. 19–20.

NOTE: *The tortillas are best eaten freshly made. If necessary, reheat them on the griddle for 15 to 30 seconds a side or wrap them 6 to 8 at a time in foil and heat in a 350°F oven for 8 to 10 minutes.*

Reheating Homemade or Store-Bought Corn or Flour Tortillas

➜ It is best to reheat tortillas individually on a griddle, 15 to 30 seconds a side or until they soften, and stack them while warm in a cloth-lined tortilla basket. If you'd like to do this step slightly ahead, you can wrap softened tortillas in a stack of 6 to 12 in foil and keep them in a 200°F oven for up to ½ hour or reheat them in a 350°F oven for about 10 minutes.

If you're using store-bought tortillas and don't have time to reheat them individually, at least separate them (the manufacturer presses them close together) before restacking them and heating in the oven in foil.

Tortillas can also be reheated between sheets of paper towels in the microwave for 1 minute.

Tortilla Chips

Totopos

**MAKES 80 CHIPS;
SERVES 6 AS AN HORS D'OEUVRE**

10 (6-inch) corn or flour tortillas

Oil

Salt

TO FRY

➜ Stack the tortillas and cut them into 8 wedges with a large knife; separate the layers. Heat 2 cups of oil in a wok or a large skillet until hot enough so that a piece of tortilla sizzles when you drop it into the oil. Fry the tortilla wedges, 8 to 12 at a time, turning with a slotted spoon until golden and crisp (the oil will stop sizzling when they are done), about 1 minute per batch. Transfer the chips to a paper-towel-lined plate to drain and sprinkle with salt.

TO BAKE

➜ Heat the oven to 350°F. Brush each tortilla lightly on both sides with oil and stack them on a cutting board. Cut them into 8 wedges each with a large knife. Separate the layers and arrange the wedges in one layer on 2 baking sheets. Bake the chips in the upper and lower thirds of the oven, switching positions halfway through, until golden and crisp, 10 to 15 minutes. Transfer the baked tortilla chips to a bowl and toss with salt.

Vegetable

There is plenty in the Mexican diet to keep vegetarians happy. You might remember from elementary school that the natives' diet hundreds of years ago was largely vegetarian, with the triumvirate of corn, beans, and squash serving as its base. Corn and beans together form a complete protein, so a corn tortilla with some refried beans is a good place to start.

One of the less familiar vegetables in some of these recipes are nopales, or cactus pads. (You might also have heard nopales referred to as prickly pear.) Fields of nopal cactuses dot the landscape near my family's house in the valley of Cuautla outside Mexico City. They are an amazing plant. Just put a pad in fertile ground and it will sprout new pads. Cut off a pad and it will grow back. On top of the pads grow cactus fruit, a vibrant, juicy fruit best turned into *agua fresca* (fruit cooler); see the recipe for one on p. 143. The pads (and fruit) do try to protect themselves with prickles, so be care-

ful when handling them. See p. 46 to learn how to remove the prickles, as well as how to cut and grill the pads, my favorite way of eating them.

Another unusual filling is corn mushrooms, called *huitlacoche* (or *cuitlacoche*). This fungus grows on the ears of corn and gradually turns the kernels into a black spongy mass that is prized for its flavor. In markets in Mexico, whole ears are displayed with their husks pulled back to reveal the delicacy within. While most farmers in the U.S. destroy crops infested with this fungus, some have caught on to its culinary uses and have brought it to farmers' markets.

Purslane (known as *verdolagas* in Mexico), while not new to the American market, is not well known. It crops up in farmers' markets in the spring and early summer, and its lemony flavor is great when lightly sautéed. It is also delicious used raw in salads or sprinkled on a mushroom taco, providing a nice contrast to the mushrooms' earthy flavor.

Spicy Refried Bean Tacos

Tacos de frijoles refritos picantes

**MAKES 1½ CUPS (4 TO
6 TACOS; SERVES 2 TO 3)**

3 tablespoons vegetable oil

1 (15-ounce) can pinto or
black beans, including liquid,
or 1½ cups cooked beans in
their liquid

½ cup Fresh Tomato Salsa
(p. 28)

1 minced chipotle en adobo,
including some liquid

1 tablespoon tequila

These refried beans are addictive, so feel free to double the
recipe (double everything except the oil, which can stay the
same). This yield is equivalent to one 15-ounce can or the
same amount of freshly cooked beans. Although the beans
make delicious tacos on their own, they also are a great
addition to beef or breakfast tacos.

Heat the oil in a medium, heavy skillet over medium heat, then
add the beans and their liquid. Mash the beans with a potato or
bean masher as they cook until their liquid is evaporated, about
5 minutes. Add the salsa, the chipotle, and the tequila and cook,
stirring or mashing until the liquid from the tomatoes has evaporated and the mixture is a fairly smooth mash, about 5 minutes.

Make tacos with accompaniments.

ACCOMPANIMENTS: *Warm tortillas, slices of avocado, more Fresh
Tomato Salsa (p. 28) or Tomatillo-Chipotle Salsa (p. 109), crumbled
queso fresco*

Fresh Tomato Salsa

Pico de gallo

MAKES 1¾ CUPS

1 cup chopped fresh toma-
toes, with seeds and juices

½ cup chopped white onion

¼ cup chopped fresh cilantro

½ jalapeño or serrano chile,
minced, or to taste

½ teaspoon salt

In the U.S. this is referred to simply as "salsa." Although most people buy it ready-made, the vibrancy of freshly homemade salsa is incomparable, and it is so simple that I strongly urge you to try it. *Pico de gallo* is especially good with vegetable or seafood tacos, though its uses are ubiquitous and need little explanation. Spoon leftover salsa on fried or scrambled eggs, as it is best to use it within a day or two.

Stir together all the ingredients and let stand for about 20 minutes for the salt to create juices before serving.

VARIATION

Simple Refried Bean Tacos

Frijoles refritos

MAKES 1½ CUPS

½ cup finely chopped white
onion

3 tablespoons vegetable oil

1 (15-ounce) can pinto or
black beans, including liquid,
or 1½ cups cooked beans in
their liquid

Salt

If you don't want as much heat as in the Spicy Refried Bean Tacos, try this instead.

Cook the onion in the oil in a medium, heavy skillet over me-dium heat, stirring, until the onion is browned on the edges, about 8 minutes. Add the beans and their liquid and cook, mashing the beans with a potato or bean masher as they cook until the liquid is evaporated and the mixture is fairly smooth, about 5 minutes. Season with salt to taste and serve with the same accompaniments as the Spicy Refried Bean Tacos (p. 27).

Swiss Chard and Potato Tacos

Tacos de acelgas y papa

**MAKES 3 CUPS (8 TO
10 TACOS; SERVES 3 TO 4)**

1 pound Swiss chard, coarse
stems removed and discarded

2 cups water

½ teaspoon salt

1 large boiling potato
(8 ounces), cut into
½-inch dice

This is a classic Mexican combination for tacos and quesadillas. The toothsome Swiss chard is rounded out by the diced
potatoes to create a simple and satisfying comfort food.

Rinse and coarsely chop the Swiss chard.

In a 3- to 4-quart pot, bring the water to a boil with the salt,
then add the potato and cook over medium heat, covered, for
5 minutes. Add the Swiss chard and cook, covered, until the chard
is crisp-tender, about 5 minutes. Drain the vegetables.

Make tacos with the accompaniments.

ACCOMPANIMENTS: *Warm corn tortillas, Tomatillo-Chipotle Salsa
(p. 109) or Fresh Tomato Salsa (p. 28), crumbled queso fresco*

Corn Mushroom Tacos

Tacos de huitlacoche

MAKES 1½ CUPS (6 TO 8 TACOS; SERVES 2 TO 3)

¼ cup chopped white onion

1 medium garlic clove, finely chopped

2 tablespoons vegetable oil or mild olive oil

2 (7.5-ounce) cans *huitlacoche,* including liquid, or 2 cups chopped fresh *huitlacoche*

2 tablespoons chopped fresh epazote leaves (optional)

Salt

Huitlacoche (also spelled *cuitlacoche*) is a mushroom that grows on corn kernels. It is considered a pest by most corn producers in the U.S., but one grower in Florida has realized its value to the Mexican community and sells it fresh in season or frozen (Burns Farms in Florida; 352-429-4048). Its earthy, almost nutty and slightly sweet flavor is deepened by the addition of epazote if you can get a hold of some fresh leaves, and in tacos it becomes a gourmet treat when topped with creamy poblano chile sauce, a slice of avocado, and crunchy onions. Canned or jarred *huitlacoche* makes an acceptable substitute for fresh and can be found at Mexican markets or ordered online from MexGrocer.com. My favorite tortillas to serve with this are the small-size magenta-tinged Hibiscus-Flavored Corn Tortillas (p. 16).

Cook the onion and garlic in the oil in a small skillet, stirring, until they are softened, about 3 minutes. Add the *huitlacoche* and epazote, if using, and simmer, stirring occasionally, until the liquid has evaporated, about 10 minutes. Season with salt to taste.

Make tacos with the accompaniments.

ACCOMPANIMENTS: *Warm corn tortillas, preferably small Hibiscus-Flavored Corn Tortillas (p. 16), chile poblano sauce (see Chicken in Poblano Chile Sauce on p. 75), avocado slices, chopped white onion*

Sauteéd Purslane Tacos

Tacos de verdolagas

MAKES 1⅓ CUPS (4 TO 6 TACOS; SERVES 2)

1½ pounds purslane, about 3 bunches, coarse bottom stems removed and discarded (tender stems are fine)

1 medium garlic clove, minced

1 tablespoon mild olive oil or vegetable oil

¼ teaspoon salt

Purslane's lovely lemony flavor is intensified in a taco with a little Cooked Tomatillo Salsa. Although you remove the tough bottom stems, it will still seem stemmy once the leaves have wilted. Don't be alarmed—it's delicious.

Rinse the purslane in plenty of cold water and drain.

Cook the garlic in the oil in a medium, heavy skillet until fragrant, about 2 minutes. Add the purslane, a large handful at a time, stirring to help wilt, and when it all fits in the skillet, cover and cook over medium-low heat for 5 minutes. Uncover and add the salt. Increase the heat and cook off any remaining liquid.

Make tacos with the accompaniments.

ACCOMPANIMENTS: *Warm corn tortillas, Cooked Tomatillo Salsa (facing page), chopped white onion, queso fresco*

MEXICAN PANTRY

Purslane

Purslane has slightly thick leaves with a lemony flavor and is available in farmers' markets in the spring and early summer. All but the tough end of the stems can be cooked. Buy a lot, as it wilts down like spinach when cooked. The tender sprigs can also be eaten raw in a salad.

Cooked Tomatillo Salsa

Salsa verde

This sauce is extremely versatile and can be added to many tacos. The unique acidity of tomatillos complements other vegetables and makes a great sauce for both meats and seafood.

MAKES 2 CUPS

1 pound tomatillos, husked and rinsed

1 to 2 serrano or jalapeño chiles, stems discarded

3 medium garlic cloves, peeled

½ teaspoon ground cumin

½ teaspoon salt

2 tablespoons vegetable oil

→ Put the tomatillos and chiles in a medium, heavy pot and cover with cold water. Bring the water to a boil, then reduce the heat and gently simmer the tomatillos and chiles, uncovered, turning them occasionally so they cook evenly, until the tomatillos are khaki-green and soft but not falling apart, about 15 minutes.

Gently lift the tomatillos and one of the chiles out of the pot and put them in the blender along with the garlic cloves, cumin, and salt. Blend until smooth. If you'd like a spicier sauce, add the other chile and blend again until smooth. Reserve the cooking water and wipe the pot dry.

Heat the oil in the dry pot over medium-high heat and carefully add the blended mixture (it may splatter). Simmer, stirring, for 5 minutes. Stir in 1 cup of the reserved cooking water and gently simmer for 5 minutes more. Check the seasoning for salt.

NOTE: *The salsa will keep in the refrigerator for 1 week.*

Guacamole Tacos

Tacos de guacamole

MAKES ABOUT 2½ CUPS (6 TO 9 TACOS; SERVES 3 TO 4)

½ cup chopped white onion, divided

½ cup chopped cilantro, divided

1 serrano or jalapeño chile, finely chopped, including the seeds

1 teaspoon kosher salt, or ½ teaspoon fine salt

2 firm-ripe avocadoes

1 cup chopped tomato, tomatillos, or fruit such as mango, peach, or apple (optional)

Avocado and salt are the two essential ingredients in any guacamole, and this simple combination makes a completely satisfying taco. If you want to add more flavor, add a chile—a chopped fresh serrano or jalapeño, with seeds please. Go a bit further and add cilantro (or experiment with other herbs like epazote) and onion. Finally, add some chopped tomato, chopped tomatillo, or even chopped fruit, and you have a full-fledged guacamole.

I don't use lime or garlic in my guacamole because they are not part of the traditional guacamole I like. What I do, though, is mash together the salt, chile, and some of the onion and cilantro before mixing with the avocado so the combination of flavors is harmonized in every bite. Coarse salt, such as kosher salt, brings together the flavors better than fine salt, but you will need a higher volume because of the size of the crystals.

Combine half of the onion and half of the cilantro on a cutting board (or in a *molcajete,* or mortar, if you have one) along with the chile and the salt. Mince together with a large knife and mash with the side of the knife to create a paste (or mash with the pestle). Transfer to a bowl. Score the avocado, twist the halves apart, and scrape the flesh out of its skin with a large spoon into the bowl. Add the remaining onion and cilantro and stir together with a fork. Stir in the tomato, tomatillo, or fruit, if using.

Make tacos with the accompaniments.

ACCOMPANIMENTS: *Warm corn tortillas, crumbled queso fresco (optional)*

VARIATION

For nonvegetarians, add some crumbled *chicharrón* (fried pork rinds) to the tacos.

Epazote

Epazote's pungent, earthy flavor makes it a great addition to mushrooms, and its digestive qualities make it a complementary ingredient for cooked beans. It is very common in Mexico and is easy to grow yourself, so add some to your kitchen garden if you like it. Whole branches can be added to simmering stocks, beans, or sauces, or the leaves can be chopped and added to finished sauces or guacamole (instead of cilantro).

Mushroom Tacos

Tacos de champiñones

MAKES 1 CUP (4 TACOS; SERVES 2)

2 tablespoons vegetable oil

1 large garlic clove, minced

½ cup chopped onion, preferably white

¼ teaspoon red pepper flakes

10 ounces mushrooms, wiped clean and sliced

2 tablespoons chopped fresh epazote leaves (optional)

½ teaspoon salt

All sorts of wild mushrooms can be found in Mexican markets, from a variety of porcini to delicately hued blue mushrooms. This recipe is written for classic button mushrooms but feel free to experiment.

Heat the oil in a large, heavy skillet, then add the garlic, onion, and red pepper flakes and cook over medium heat, stirring, until slightly softened, about 3 minutes. Stir in the mushrooms, cover the pan, and cook, stirring occasionally, until the mushrooms are wilted and have given off their juices, about 5 minutes. Uncover and add the epazote leaves, if using, and salt and cook, stirring, until most of the liquid has evaporated, about 5 minutes.

Make tacos with the accompaniments.

ACCOMPANIMENTS: *Warm corn tortillas, Tomatillo-Chipotle Salsa (p. 109) or Fresh Tomato Salsa (p. 28), crumbled queso fresco (optional)*

Spinach and Mushroom Tacos

Remove the coarse stems from 1 pound of fresh spinach and wash the leaves. Bring 1 cup of water to a boil in a medium pot and add the spinach. Cover and cook until wilted, stirring occasionally, about 5 minutes. Drain the spinach and when cool enough to handle, squeeze out the excess water. Coarsely chop the spinach. Follow the directions for making Mushroom Tacos, stirring the spinach into the cooked mushroom mixture. Serve tacos with Roasted Tomato-Serrano Salsa (p. 145).

Mushroom and Poblano Chile Tacos

Add ½ cup poblano chile strips (from 1 large chile; see the sidebar on p. 41 for how to roast poblano chiles) to the pan along with the raw mushrooms and cook as directed for Mushroom Tacos. Serve tacos with Roasted Tomato-Serrano Salsa (p. 145) or Tomatillo-Chipotle Salsa (p. 109) and queso fresco.

Fried Avocado Tacos

Tacos de aguacate rebosado

MAKES 12 TACOS; SERVES 4

3 to 4 cups vegetable oil for frying

1 cup (8 ounces) beer

½ teaspoon salt

1 cup flour

3 firm-ripe avocadoes, quartered, pitted, and peeled

Frying avocadoes may seem as strange to you as they did to me until I tasted them at Puntarena in Mexico City. They are a delight, so give them a try! Combine them with Delicate Fried Shrimp Tacos (p. 62) or Grilled Garlic-Marinated Skirt Steak Tacos (p. 121).

➡ Heat the oil in a 4-quart pot or a wok until a deep-fat thermometer registers 360°F.

Put the beer in a wide bowl and stir in the salt. Put the flour in another wide bowl.

Cut each quarter of avocado into 3 long wedges and dunk the wedges first in the beer, then turn them gently in the flour to coat.

Transfer about 6 avocado slices at a time to the oil and fry until a light-golden crust forms, 1 to 2 minutes. Transfer to a paper-towel-lined plate to drain. Fry more avocado slices in the same manner until all slices have been fried.

Make tacos with 3 slices of avocado and the accompaniments.

ACCOMPANIMENTS: *Warm flour or corn tortillas, Lime-Chipotle Mayonnaise (p. 54), chopped cilantro*

Creamy Poblano Chile and Corn Tacos

Tacos de rajas de chile poblano con elote

**MAKES 3 CUPS (9 TO
12 TACOS; SERVES 4 TO 5)**

1 pound fresh poblano chiles
(4 to 8); see p. 57

1 medium white onion, sliced
lengthwise into thin strips

¼ cup vegetable oil

1 cup frozen and thawed or
roasted corn kernels (see
Roasted Corn Salsa on p. 76)

½ teaspoon salt; more to
taste

¾ cup Mexican crema, crème
fraîche, or sour cream

Roasted poblano chiles and corn have a natural affinity—the
sweetness of the corn balances the pleasant bitterness
and heat of the poblano chiles. Without the corn this recipe
becomes *rajas con crema*, a classic addition to grilled
beef tacos.

Char the chiles directly on the flames of the stovetop with the
heat at medium high (see p. 41).

Transfer the chiles to a bowl and let stand, covered with a plate
or plastic wrap, to loosen the skins, at least 15 minutes. Peel the
chiles, then slit them open and remove and discard the seeds,
seed pod, and veins. Cut the chiles into ⅓-inch-wide strips.

In a heavy skillet cook the onion in the oil over medium-low
heat, stirring frequently, until softened, about 5 minutes. Add
the corn and salt and cook, stirring, until the corn is just cooked
through (or reheated if precooked). Add the chiles and cook, stirring, for 2 minutes. Stir in the crema and heat through without
boiling. Season with salt to taste.

Make tacos with the accompaniments.

ACCOMPANIMENTS: *Warm corn tortillas, avocado slices, lime
wedges, queso fresco or feta cheese*

VARIATIONS

Rajas con Crema

Omit the corn in Creamy Poblano Chile and Corn Tacos.

Rajas

Omit the corn and the cream in Creamy Poblano Chile and
Corn Tacos.

Roasting and Cleaning a Poblano Chile

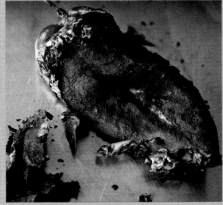

Char the poblano chile directly on the flames of a burner with the heat at medium high (you can do this directly on a gas or electric burner), turning the chile with tongs as it blackens, until it is blackened all over, 6 to 8 minutes.

After putting the roasted chile in a plastic bag to sweat for 15 minutes, rub off the charred skin with a paper towel or your fingers. Alternatively, put the chile in a bowl and cover with plastic wrap.

Slit the chile open, cut out the seed pod with scissors, and remove and discard the remaining seeds and veins.

Cut the chile into ⅓-inch-wide strips.

Tacos with Cheese-Stuffed Ancho Chiles

Chiles anchos rellenos de queso

MAKES 16 TACOS; SERVES 6 TO 8

FOR THE CHILES

8 small ancho chiles
(2 ounces total)

½ pound shredded Oaxaca, mozzarella, or Monterey Jack cheese

FOR THE TOMATO SAUCE

1 (14- to 15-ounce) can whole tomatoes in juice

¼ cup chopped white onion

2 large garlic cloves

1 tablespoon distilled white vinegar

1 tablespoon sugar

1 teaspoon dried crumbled oregano, preferably Mexican

¾ teaspoon salt

2 tablespoons corn oil or other vegetable oil

FOR THE EGG COATING AND FRYING

¼ cup flour

2 cups corn oil or other vegetable oil

3 large eggs, separated

¼ teaspoon salt

This recipe is a great way to use small ancho chiles. Even so, they have to be cut in half before serving, since the egg coating they are fried in makes them too large. Gustavo Millan, owner of Tacos Gus in Mexico (one of my favorite spots in Mexico City), serves them bathed in the traditional mild tomato sauce, but I think they become too wet for a taco. Here, serve them with the thickened sauce on the side to add to the tacos.

If you want a hotter sauce, add a serrano to the blender when making the sauce.

SOAK AND STUFF THE CHILES

Put the chiles in a heat-proof bowl and cover with boiling water. Let stand until softened, about 20 minutes. Drain.

Cut a slit lengthwise in each chile and carefully remove the seed pod without tearing the chile. Stuff the chiles with the cheese and close them up, overlapping the slit slightly if possible.

MAKE THE TOMATO SAUCE

Combine all of the sauce ingredients except the oil in a blender and blend until smooth.

Heat the oil in a 3- to 4-quart heavy pot over medium-high heat until hot but not smoking. Quickly and carefully pour in the sauce (it will splatter) and simmer, stirring occasionally, until thickened, about 10 minutes. Transfer to a bowl and set aside.

COAT AND FRY THE CHILES

Put the flour in a wide bowl. Working with 1 chile at a time, dredge the chile with flour, keeping the slit in the chile closed as you coat it. Knock off the excess flour and transfer to a plate.

In a 12-inch, heavy skillet slowly heat the oil until hot.

While the oil is heating, beat the egg whites and salt with an electric mixer on medium speed until soft peaks form. Gently fold in the yolks with a rubber spatula.

When the oil is hot, working in batches, hold one chile at a time by the stem and dip in the egg coating, using the rubber spatula to help cover the chile completely, then transfer it, still holding it by the stem, to the oil. Fry 4 chiles at a time in the oil, turning once, until golden on all sides (spoon hot oil over any lighter areas as you fry), about 4 minutes per batch. With a slotted spoon, transfer the fried chiles to a paper-towel-lined plate to drain. Continue until all chiles are fried.

Cut off the stems and cut the chiles in half lengthwise so they fit the tacos; arrange on a plate.

Make tacos with the corn tortillas and the tomato sauce.

ACCOMPANIMENT: *Warm corn tortillas*

VARIATION

Stuffed Ancho Chiles with Green Sauce

Instead of making the tomato sauce, serve the chiles with Cooked Tomatillo Salsa (p. 33).

MEXICAN PANTRY

Oaxaca Cheese

Oaxaca cheese is a white cow's milk string cheese, more toothsome and with a higher melting point than mozzarella. Wide ribbons of cheese are wrapped in a ball like a ball of wool. It is available in Latino markets and some supermarkets that carry Mexican ingredients. When I buy it fresh from a market in Oaxaca, Mexico, it is hard to resist unraveling the ribbons and eating it right away. Armenian string cheese, often found in American supermarkets, is very similar in texture although the nigella seeds Oaxaca is sprinkled with give it a different flavor.

Grilled Cactus Pad Tacos

Tacos de nopal

**MAKES 2 CUPS (8 TO
10 TACOS; SERVES 3)**

4 nopal cactus pads (about
5 ounces each)

Vegetable or mild olive oil for
brushing

Salt for sprinkling

My favorite way of cooking nopales, or prickly pear, is grilling
them, which brings out a lovely deep herbal flavor. Complete
the taco with some *pico de gallo* and queso fresco and you're
in for a treat. Nopales, found in most Latino markets, are
often sold with the prickles already removed, but if not, you
can do it yourself (see p. 46).

➡ Heat a grill or a grill pan.

Remove the prickles from the cactus pads by running a knife
horizontal to the pad in the same direction as the prickles (see the
sidebar on p. 46). Make about 3 lengthwise cuts from the thick end
of the cactus pads to the middle so they cook evenly, then brush
the pads with oil and sprinkle with salt.

Grill the pads for 3 to 4 minutes a side until grill marks appear
and the pads have changed color, which indicates they are cooked.

Cut the pads in half lengthwise, then cut crosswise into strips.

Make tacos with the accompaniments.

ACCOMPANIMENTS: *Warm corn tortillas, Fresh Tomato Salsa
(p. 28), crumbled queso fresco*

Removing Prickles from Nopal Cactus Pads

With a large knife, cut the prickles from both sides of the pads, working from the thicker base to the top. Cut a thin strip from the edges of the pads to remove the prickles there.

Make two to three cuts through the thick base so that the leaves cook evenly when grilled. Don't cut through to the top of the pad. Lightly brush them with oil before grilling.

Squash, Tomato, and Onion Tacos

Tacos de milpa

**MAKES 3 CUPS (10 TO
12 TACOS; SERVES 3 TO 4)**

1 cup chopped white onion

2 large garlic cloves, chopped

3 tablespoons mild olive oil

1¼ pounds *calabacitas* or
zucchini, scrubbed and cut
into ½-inch dice

2 medium tomatoes
(10 ounces), diced

¼ cup chopped fresh epazote
or cilantro

½ teaspoon salt

4 ounces grated Monterey
Jack cheese (1¼ cups)

A *milpa* is a Mexican kitchen garden that includes squash, tomatoes, and onions. The squash called for are *calabacitas*, a Mexican vegetable similar to zucchini, with lighter green skin. They come in both long and round shapes and can be found in Latino markets. Enriched with a little cheese, these tacos are heartwarming vegetarian fare.

Cook the onion and garlic in the oil in a 3- to 4-quart heavy pot over medium heat, stirring, until softened, about 3 minutes. Stir in the *calabacitas* or zucchini, tomatoes, epazote or cilantro, and salt, then cover the pot and cook for 5 minutes. Uncover and cook, stirring occasionally, until any liquid is reduced. Add the cheese and stir until it is melted.

Make tacos with the accompaniments.

ACCOMPANIMENTS: *Warm corn tortillas, Cooked Tomatillo Salsa (p. 33) or Poblano Chile Sauce (p. 75), crumbled queso fresco*

Tacos with Melted Cheese and Poblano Strips

Tacos de queso fundido con rajas

MAKES 6 TACOS; SERVES 2

1 poblano chile

4 ounces Monterey Jack cheese, or a mixture of Monterey Jack, Oaxaca, and Manchego cheeses, grated (1⅓ cups)

Baby cast-iron skillets or individual baking dishes, like ceramic Spanish dishes, are great for baking and serving the melted cheese. This recipe features poblano chile strips, but other popular additions are cooked mushrooms or cooked crumbled chorizo. The quantities here assume 1 individual baking dish serves 2. Make another dishful for each additional 2 people, so it is easy for everyone to make their own tacos.

Char the poblano chile directly on the flames of a burner with the heat at medium-high (you can do this directly on a gas or electric burner), turning it with tongs, until it is blackened all over, 6 to 8 minutes. (For more on this, see p. 41.)

Transfer the chile to a plastic bag to sweat for 15 minutes. Remove the charred skin from the chile, then slit open the chile and remove and discard the seeds, seed pod, and veins. Cut the chile into 2-inch-wide by ¼-inch-thick strips.

Heat the oven to 350°F.

Put the cheese and the chile strips in a small ovenproof dish and bake in the oven until the cheese is melted and bubbling, 5 to 8 minutes.

Make tacos with the accompaniments.

NOTE: *The poblano strips can be made ahead and chilled for up to 3 days.*

ACCOMPANIMENT: *Warm corn tortillas*

Seafood

Since Mexico has nearly 6,000 miles of coastline on two oceans and two seas, it is not surprising that seafood was one of the principle sources of protein in pre-Hispanic Mexico, before the conquerors brought the domesticated animals. Today, fish markets still display an extensive variety of fish and seafood, with the local catch differing from region to region.

Fish markets along the Caribbean coast of the Yucatan peninsula are rich with the exotic fish of the extensive Alacranes Reef system. Baby shark, a local specialty, is cooked and shredded into tacos.

The city of Campeche, at the foot of the Gulf of Mexico, is a major exporter of seafood—most notably shrimp, which plays an important part in the local economy. Around Mexico, the seafood cocktail known as "Campechana" means a variety of seafood and includes a mix of oysters, baby octopus, mussels, squid, scallops, and shrimp. Typically this cocktail is served chilled in a tall glass with a spoon.

Small fishing boats in Zihuatanejo, on the central Pacific coast, come back loaded with the local small tuna, called bonito, as well as the ubiquitous red snapper (caught on both coasts) and dorado (mahimahi). The local dish of *tiritas*—mahimahi strips marinated in lime juice, olive oil, and oregano with onions—is made from the bounty of these expeditions.

Baja, which has become famous for its fish, shrimp, and lobster tacos, is abundantly supplied by both the Sea of Cortez (Gulf of California) and the Pacific.

Veracruz, as the port of entry of the Spanish Conquest, shows a very strong Spanish influence in its extensive variety of seafood dishes, with the presence of olive oil, olives, and capers.

The recipes in this chapter show some of this variety as well as introduce contemporary dishes being served by some of Mexico's current culinary leaders.

Baja Fish Tacos

MAKES ABOUT 20 TACOS; SERVES 6

FOR THE BATTER

1 cup all-purpose flour

1 teaspoon salt

1 cup (8 ounces) beer

FOR THE FISH

3 to 4 cups vegetable oil for frying

1 pound tilapia, cod, or other white fish fillets

½ teaspoon salt

1 cup flour

While fish dishes with tomatoes, olives, and capers are emblematic of the Veracruz coast, these battered fried tacos are typical of the Baja peninsula. A little shredded cabbage mixed with chipotle mayonnaise adds just the right crunch and spice.

MAKE THE BATTER

Whisk together the batter ingredients and let stand for 15 minutes.

COOK THE FISH

Heat the oil in a 4-quart pot or a wok until a deep-fat thermometer registers 375°F.

While the oil is heating, cut the fish into ½- by 4-inch strips and toss with the salt. Place the flour in a wide, shallow bowl. Dredge the fish in the flour, then in the batter, and fry a few pieces at a time, until the batter is golden and the fish is just cooked through, 3 to 4 minutes. Transfer the fish to a paper-towel-lined plate to drain.

Make tacos with the accompaniments.

NOTE: *If you have a wok for deep-frying, you can use less oil, 2 to 3 cups.*

ACCOMPANIMENTS: *Warm corn tortillas, some Lime-Chipotle Mayonnaise (see p. 54) mixed with shredded cabbage; serve the rest of the mayonnaise on the side along with lime wedges*

Lime-Chipotle Mayonnaise

MAKES 1 CUP

1 cup mayonnaise

3 tablespoons *chipotles en adobo*, finely chopped, including the sauce

1 tablespoon lime juice

→ Mix together all the ingredients.

If you'd like to thin the sauce for drizzling, add a little water to the mixture.

Tacos with Chopped Fish and Tomatillo "Salad"

Tacos de Salpićon de pescado rigoletti

MAKES 4 CUPS (8 TO 12 TACOS; SERVES 4)

FOR THE FISH

1 pound mahimahi fillets in one or two pieces

½ teaspoon salt

½ teaspoon black pepper

⅓ cup mild olive oil

FOR THE DRESSING

¼ cup lime juice

1 tablespoon minced *chipotles en adobo*

½ tablespoon Worcestershire sauce

1 teaspoon dried oregano, preferably Mexican

½ teaspoon salt

¼ cup extra-virgin olive oil

FOR THE "SALAD"

3 large tomatillos, husked, rinsed, and coarsely chopped

1 cup chopped white onion

2 large jalapeños, seeded and chopped

1 cup coarsely chopped cilantro

Chef Federico Rigoletti is a master of fish preparations and has several restaurants in Mexico City, most notably Puntarena, that specialize in fish dishes. I asked him to prepare some fish tacos for me and he created this dish. *Salpicón* means any chopped mixture, and here Chef Rigoletti uses raw tomatillos for a modern but very Mexican interpretation. Be sure the fish is well browned so that it has a crunchy crust.

COOK THE FISH

Pat the fish dry with paper towels and season with salt and pepper. Heat the oil in a medium, heavy skillet over medium-high heat until hot, then add the fish and cook on each side until a golden-brown crust forms, about 7 minutes total. Transfer to a cutting board and coarsely chop.

MAKE THE DRESSING

Whisk together everything except the olive oil in a bowl, then slowly whisk in the olive oil.

MAKE THE FISH SALAD

In a large bowl, combine the chopped fish, tomatillo, onion, and jalapeños. Add the dressing and toss to distribute. Just before serving stir in the cilantro.

Make tacos with the accompaniments.

ACCOMPANIMENTS: *Warm flour tortillas, sliced avocado*

VARIATION

Make tostadas with this salad. Heat 4 tortillas (homemade black bean or store-bought corn) in ½ cup vegetable oil until golden and crisp, about 1 minute each; drain. Top with the salad.

Fresh Chiles

As a general rule, the smaller the chile the hotter it is. Of the chiles pictured the hottest is the habanero and the mildest is the poblano. However, no two chiles are alike, so the best way to evaluate the heat of a chile is to cut it open and smell it. Be careful not to get the chile near your eyes, and do not touch your eyes after you have touched the cut edge of a chile.

1. manzano 2. jalapeño 3. habanero 4. serrano and 5. poblano

Asian Tuna Tacos

Tacos de atún estilo japones

MAKES 8 TO 12 TACOS; SERVES 4

FOR THE WASABI MAYONNAISE

½ cup mayonnaise

1 tablespoon prepared wasabi, or 2 tablespoons powdered wasabi mixed with 1 teaspoon water

2 teaspoons soy sauce

2 teaspoons lime juice

½ teaspoon sugar

FOR THE TUNA

1 pound tuna steaks, about 1 inch thick

½ teaspoon salt

½ cup unhulled sesame seeds

3 tablespoons mild olive oil

This is a nod to the popularity of Japanese food, in particular sushi, in Mexico City. Here, tuna steaks are seared with a sesame seed crust and served with a wasabi mayonnaise, chopped scallions, and cilantro or the more exotic radish sprouts. Flour tortillas are used because they are a more neutral background to the tuna.

MAKE THE MAYONNAISE

Stir together all ingredients and taste to check seasoning.

PREPARE THE TUNA

Pat the tuna dry with paper towels and season with the salt.

Put the sesame seeds on a plate and press both flat sides of the tuna steaks onto the seeds to coat.

Heat a large, heavy skillet over medium-high heat until hot, about 2 minutes. Add the oil and swirl the pan to distribute, then add the tuna steaks, in batches if necessary, and sear for about 2 minutes each side, until just the outside ¼ inch is cooked but the center is still translucent.

Transfer the tuna steaks to a cutting board and slice. Make tacos with the wasabi mayonnaise and accompaniments.

ACCOMPANIMENTS: *Warm flour tortillas, chopped scallions, radish sprouts, or chopped cilantro, sliced avocado*

MEXICAN PANTRY

Sesame Seeds

Sesame seeds used in Mexican cooking are unhulled. They are tan colored rather than the pearly white hulled ones that are typical in the U.S., and can be bought in any market that carries Mexican ingredients.

Broiled Fish Steak Tacos

Tacos de pescado

MAKES ABOUT 16 LARGE TACOS; SERVES 6 TO 8

Oil

2 pounds 1-inch-thick sword-fish or mahimahi steaks

1 teaspoon salt

1 cup Smoky Adobo Mayonnaise (below)

The very flavorful mayonnaise makes this broiled fish a fast taco treat.

→ Heat a broiler and line the rack of a broiler pan with foil. Oil the foil.

Pat the fish steaks dry with paper towels and season with the salt. Put them on the foil and slather thickly with the mayonnaise.

Broil the steaks about 5 or 6 inches from the heat until they are just cooked through and the topping is golden, about 8 minutes.

Coarsely chop the fish; make tacos with the accompaniments.

ACCOMPANIMENTS: *Warm corn or flour tortillas, avocado slices, lime wedges*

Smoky Adobo Mayonnaise

Mayonesa de adobo

MAKES ABOUT 2 CUPS

1 ounce guajillo chiles (4 large), wiped clean, seeded, and deveined

2 ounces ancho chiles (4 large), wiped clean, seeded, and deveined

3 medium tomatoes

Two ½-inch-thick slices of white onion

6 large garlic cloves, unpeeled

5 *chipotles en adobo*, seeds removed

½ cup mayonnaise

Roberto Craig of Primos restaurant in Mexico City uses this as a thick marinade for broiling seafood and chicken. It keeps a long time in the fridge—about 3 weeks—so it's great to have on hand to put together a quick meal. Roberto uses dried chipotles instead of the *chipotles en adobo* called for here; if you can get them, treat them like the other chiles.

→ Soak the dried chiles in a bowl of cold water to cover and let sit until softened, about 20 minutes. Drain.

While the chiles are soaking, heat an oven or a toaster oven to 500°F and line a baking pan with foil. Core the tomatoes and cut an X through the skin on the opposite end. Arrange the onion slices, garlic cloves, and tomatoes on the foil, cored side up. Roast until the garlic is just tender with some brown spots, about

15 minutes, the onion is browned and softened, about 20 minutes, turning once, and the tomatoes are blackened and tender, 25 to 30 minutes. Peel the garlic.

Blend the drained chiles with the roasted onion, garlic, and tomatoes, as well as the *chipotles en adobo* and mayonnaise, adding just enough water to blend the mixture and keep the sauce thick.

MEXICAN PANTRY

Chipotle Chiles

"Chipotle" means smoked, and there are two main kinds of chipotle chiles, which start out as jalapeño chiles. Chipotle meco chiles are large (1 inch by 3 to 4 inches), tobacco-colored chiles while chipotle morita chiles are smaller (1 inch by 2 inches) and a deep reddish-purple color. They are both very spicy. *Chipotles en adobo* are made from the smaller chipotle morita chiles. If you can't find them in your local market or Latin grocery, they can be ordered online from www. sweetfreedomfarm.com.

Delicate Fried Shrimp Tacos

**MAKES 6 TO 9 TACOS;
SERVES 2 TO 3**

3 to 4 cups vegetable oil for
deep frying

1 pound medium shrimp
(30 to 35), peeled and
deveined

1 teaspoon salt

1 cup (8 ounces) beer

1 cup flour

2 cups flat-leaf parsley leaves

This deconstructed "batter," the creation of chef Federico Rigoletti (of Puntarena restaurant in Mexico City), gives the shrimp the lightest possible coating while still imparting some of the typical beer flavor. Federico finishes off his shrimp tacos with either deep-fried parsley leaves or a slice of similarly fried avocado (p. 38).

Heat the oil in a 4-quart pot or a wok until a deep-fat thermometer registers 360°F.

Toss the shrimp with the salt and let stand to season, 5 to 10 minutes.

Put the beer in a bowl and add the shrimp. Put the flour in another bowl.

With a slotted spoon, transfer a few shrimp at a time to the flour and toss to coat. Put them in a medium-mesh sieve and toss to knock off excess flour.

Working in batches, put the shrimp in the oil and cook, turning as necessary, until the coating is pale golden and the shrimp are just cooked, 2 to 3 minutes. Just before the shrimp are finished cooking add a few parsley leaves and cook for a few seconds, or until the bubbles subside. Transfer to a paper-towel-lined plate to drain.

Continue cooking shrimp and parsley in batches.

Make tacos with the accompaniments.

NOTE: *If you have a wok for deep-frying you can use less oil, 2 to 3 cups.*

ACCOMPANIMENTS: *Warm flour or corn tortillas, Lime-Chipotle Mayonnaise (p. 54) mixed with some shredded cabbage if desired, lime wedges*

Tacos with Grilled Shrimp in Adobo

Tacos de Camarones en adobo a la parilla

**MAKES 8 TO 10 TACOS;
SERVES 3 TO 4**

1 pound medium shrimp
(30 to 35), peeled and
deveined

½ teaspoon salt

⅓ cup Adobo Marinade
(p. 128)

Metal skewers or soaked
bamboo skewers

The dried chile sauce called "adobo" is a Mexican version of a barbecue sauce and works just as well for marinating seafood as for marinating meat. The marinade can be frozen for about a month, so keep some on hand for quick meals like this.

➡ Toss the shrimp in a bowl with the salt, then add the Adobo Marinade and toss to coat.

Thread shrimp onto the skewers and chill on a tray covered with plastic wrap for at least 20 minutes and up to 2 hours. (You can chill them before threading them onto the skewers if you prefer.)

Prepare a grill or heat a grill pan. Grill the shrimp until just cooked through, about 2 minutes a side.

Remove the shrimp from the skewers and make tacos with the accompaniments, using 3 to 4 shrimp per taco.

ACCOMPANIMENTS: *Warm corn tortillas, avocado slices, chopped onion, chopped cilantro, more Adobo Marinade to drizzle on top. Alternatively, serve the shrimp with Mango-Habanero Salsa (p. 65).*

Lobster and Mango Salsa Tacos

Tacos de langosta con salsa de mango

MAKES ABOUT 4 LARGE TACOS; SERVES 2

One 2- to 2½-pound lobster

1 recipe Mango-Habanero Salsa (below)

The sweet and spicy salsa enhances the sweetness of the lobster meat in this supereasy taco.

Bring a large pot of water to a boil and plunge the lobster head first into the water. Boil for 9 minutes. Remove the lobster and let cool.

Remove the meat from the body and the claws (see the sidebar on p. 66) and coarsely chop. You will have about 1½ cups of lobster meat.

Make tacos with the salsa.

ACCOMPANIMENT: *Warm flour or corn tortillas*

Mango-Habanero Salsa

MAKES ABOUT 1¾ CUPS

1 cup diced mango

½ cup chopped red onion

¼ cup chopped cilantro

½ chopped fresh habanero chile

2 tablespoons lime juice

¼ teaspoon salt

Fruit salsas go especially well with seafood tacos because they bring out the sweetness of the meat. All you need is some boiled or grilled shrimp or lobster and you have a delicious and refreshing meal. If you find fresh habanero chiles, buy a bunch and freeze them in a tightly sealed plastic bag (they'll keep for 3 months in the freezer). If you can't find them, substitute a fresh serrano or jalapeño chile.

Stir all the ingredients together in a bowl.

NOTE: *The mango salsa is best eaten the day it is made.*

Removing Lobster Meat from the Shell

→ To remove lobster meat from the shell, start with the tail and twist it off the body of the lobster. Bend the tail fins upward until they snap off. Use your finger to push the tail meat out of the shell. Make a shallow incision down the center top of the tail to expose the intestinal tract. Flick out the tract with the tip of the knife and discard.

Separate the knuckles and claws from the body in one piece by twisting them off or cutting with shears. Separate the knuckles from the claws. Crack open the knuckles with the back of a chef's knife or cut them open with shears. Remove the nuggets of meat.

To get the meat from the claws, bend the small part of the claw up and down until it snaps. Gently pull away this small shell, leaving the meat inside still attached to the big part of the claw. With shears or the back of a chef's knife, crack open the claw and remove the meat in one piece.

Octopus Tacos with Pickled Jalapeños, Olives, and Capers

Tacos de salpicón de pulpo

**MAKES ABOUT 3 CUPS
(ABOUT 9 TACOS; SERVES 3)**

FOR THE OCTOPUS

One 1- to 1½-pound octopus, thawed if frozen

½ white onion, sliced

2 bay leaves

2 teaspoons salt

FOR THE *SALPICÓN*

2 tablespoons olive oil

1 cup chopped white onion

3 medium garlic cloves, minced

1 pound tomatoes (3 medium), seeded and chopped

½ teaspoon salt

2 tablespoons green olives, pitted and chopped

2 pickled jalapeños, chopped

2 tablespoons capers

These tacos are native to the coast of Veracruz, where seasonings are heavily influenced by ingredients from the Spanish *conquista*, as Veracruz was the port of entry. Olives, capers, and olive oil are commonly used here and are best known in the famous fish Pescado a la Veracruzana. Perhaps that is where the pickled ingredients in this taco had their first marriage with the native tomato, which is the basis of the sauce in both dishes.

Octopi vary greatly in size and therefore cooking time. If you can get a small one, 1 to 1½ pounds, it will cook in about 45 minutes; a larger one, 3 to 5 pounds, can take as long as 1½ to 2 hours. Increase the *salpicón* ingredients accordingly.

COOK THE OCTOPUS

Remove the hard beak from the octopus, if necessary. Bring 2 quarts water to a boil in a large saucepan with the onion, bay leaves, and salt. Using tongs, dunk the octopus in the boiling water for a few seconds three times (this will help keep the purple skin on the cooked octopus), then immerse the octopus in the water and simmer until a fork pierces the thicker part of the tentacles easily, about 45 minutes.

Remove the octopus, and when cool enough to handle, slice the tentacles into ½-inch pieces.

MAKE THE *SALPICÓN*

Heat the olive oil in a large skillet over medium heat and cook the onion and garlic, stirring, until softened, 3 to 5 minutes. Add the tomatoes and salt and cook, stirring occasionally, until the tomatoes start to dissolve into a sauce, 3 to 5 minutes. Add the octopus to the skillet along with the olives, pickled jalapeños, and capers and cook, stirring, until everything is heated through.

Make tacos with warm tortillas.

ACCOMPANIMENT: *Warm corn tortillas*

Seared Scallop Tacos with Jicama-Peanut Slaw

Callo de hacha con pico de piñata

MAKES 8 TO 10 TACOS; SERVES 3 TO 4

FOR THE *PICO DE PIÑATA*

1 cup diced (¼ inch) jicama

2 large clementines or 1 navel orange, peeled, including all white pit, and diced (1 cup) plus juice from 1 large clementine or ½ navel orange

½ cup chopped red onion

½ cup chopped *chicharrón* (fried pork skin) (optional)

¼ cup chopped cocktail peanuts

¼ cup chopped cilantro

1 habanero chile, minced

¼ teaspoon salt

FOR THE SCALLOPS

1 pound sea scallops, tough ligaments removed

1 teaspoon salt

1 tablespoon vegetable or olive oil

This is a departure from classic Mexican tacos and is inspired by a chef of modern Mexican cooking, Enrique Olvera, who serves foie gras with this *pico* at his Mexico City restaurant, Pujol. This dish is called *"pico de piñata"* because many of the ingredients—the clementines, jicama, and peanuts—are traditionally stuffed inside a piñata.

MAKE THE *PICO DE PIÑATA*

Stir together all the ingredients in a bowl.

COOK THE SCALLOPS

Heat a large, heavy skillet over medium-high heat until hot.

While the skillet is heating, pat the scallops dry with paper towels and season them with salt.

Add the oil to the skillet and swirl to coat the bottom. Immediately add the scallops, one by one so they aren't touching, and cook, without moving, until the undersides are browned, about 3 minutes (when the scallops are ready they will move when you shake the pan because their browned crust will release them from the pan). Turn the scallops over and cook until just cooked through, about 2 minutes more.

Cut the scallops into ½-inch pieces and make tacos with the *pico de piñata*.

ACCOMPANIMENT: *Warm flour or corn tortillas*

VARIATION

Substitute popcorn shrimp for the scallops. Season with salt and sauté, stirring, until just cooked through, 2 to 3 minutes.

Chicken,
Turkey, and Duck

The native fowl of Mexico included duck and turkey, but chickens were brought by the Spaniards. They are now the most widely consumed form of animal protein in Mexico. Since ovens are a fairly modern invention, chickens have commonly been boiled in water, producing a soul-satisfying broth to add to the sauces it is served with.

Sauces are not to be underestimated in Mexican cooking. Partly because meat, even chicken, can be expensive and partly because so much effort and artistry goes into them, sauces are the main event. It is a testament to Mexican ingenuity that such an immense variety of sauces exist. Mole poblano, a harmonious blending of nuts, seeds, dried chiles, spices, and fruit, is famously considered the most complex. Like many moles, it works well with all types of poultry.

A lesser-known and simpler sauce I have included is a poblano chile sauce. Don't confuse the two.

Mole poblano is named after the town and state it originated in, Puebla. The fresh chile is also named after Puebla but is not an ingredient in the mole.

For tacos, chicken is usually shredded and added to the sauce, which is made separately. For some of these recipes, I have cut raw chicken into cubes and sautéed them because I find the texture more satisfying in a taco. If you prefer, you could also quickly grill thinly pounded chicken breasts and chop them up to serve with the sauces in this chapter as well as the salsas scattered throughout the book.

The Duck Legs Braised in Chipotle-Tomatillo Sauce (p. 87) is one of my favorite tacos in the chapter, up there with the Yucatecan Pulled Pork Tacos (p. 103) in the Pork chapter, the Grilled Cactus Pad Tacos (p. 44) in the Vegetable chapter, and the Grilled Garlic-Marinated Skirt Steak Tacos (p. 121) in the Meat chapter.

Tacos with Shredded Chicken and Onion

Tacos de pollo

MAKES 5 CUPS (15 TO 18 TACOS; SERVES 5 TO 6)

1 large white onion, finely chopped (1½ cups)

¼ cup vegetable oil or mild olive oil

1 roasted or Poached Chicken (p. 74), meat shredded (about 4 cups)

2 teaspoons dried oregano, preferably Mexican

1 teaspoon dried thyme, or 1 tablespoon chopped fresh thyme

Salt

Give a boost to shredded chicken with these simple seasonings—onion, oregano, and thyme. Guacamole serves as a mild salsa in these tacos, but feel free to use any other salsa you like.

➡ Cook the onion in the oil in a large skillet over medium heat until slightly softened, about 2 minutes. Stir in the chicken, oregano, thyme, and salt to taste and cook, stirring, until heated through, 3 to 5 minutes.

Make tacos with the accompaniments.

ACCOMPANIMENTS: *Warm corn tortillas, guacamole (p. 34)*

Poached Chicken and Chicken Stock

MAKES 5 CUPS SHREDDED CHICKEN AND ABOUT 2 QUARTS CHICKEN STOCK

1 whole chicken (3½ pounds), cut into serving pieces (or 3½ pounds chicken parts)

2½ quarts water

1 white onion, quartered

6 medium garlic cloves, peeled

3 large cilantro sprigs

3 bay leaves

10 black peppercorns

1 teaspoon salt

Typically meat and chicken are cooked in water to provide both meat for the main dish and stock for making the sauces that are the main focus of most Mexican dishes. Store-bought rotisserie chicken can also be used in these recipes, but you will need broth as well. Make sure the roasting pot is big enough to hold water to cover the meat.

➡ Put the chicken in a 6- to 8-quart pot with the remaining ingredients and bring to a simmer over high heat, skimming any foam from the surface as necessary. Reduce the heat and simmer until the chicken is just cooked through, about 30 minutes.

Remove the chicken pieces from the stock. When they're cool enough to handle, remove the skin from the chicken and shred the meat.

Strain the stock into a large, wide bowl, discarding the vegetables.

NOTE: *The chicken and chicken stock can be kept chilled (cool completely first) for 3 days or frozen for up to 6 months.*

VARIATION

Poached Turkey

➡ Poach a 3- to 4-pound turkey breast or thighs in the same manner. Thighs will take about 45 minutes to cook through.

Tacos with Chicken in Poblano Chile Sauce

Tacos de pollo en salsa de chile poblano

MAKES 5 CUPS (15 TO 18 TACOS; SERVES 5 TO 6)

FOR THE SAUCE

1 pound fresh poblano chiles (4 to 8)

¾ cup chopped white onion

2 large garlic cloves, minced

1 tablespoon vegetable oil

½ teaspoon salt

½ cup homemade chicken stock or canned chicken broth

FOR THE CHICKEN

2 pounds boneless, skinless chicken breasts, cut into ½-inch cubes

1 teaspoon salt

2 tablespoons vegetable oil

I had chicken in a poblano chile sauce for the first time in the charming mountain town of Cuetzálan, Puebla. It was so delicious I was surprised I hadn't had it before. When I looked for recipes and couldn't find one, I was told by my Mexican friends that it was so simple that no one bothers to write it down. If you are a poblano chile lover, this is the sauce for you.

MAKE THE SAUCE

➡ Char the chiles directly on the flames of a gas stovetop with the heat at medium-high (you can do this directly on electric burners as well), turning them with tongs as they blacken until they are blackened all over, 6 to 8 minutes (see the sidebar on p. 41).

Transfer the chiles to a bowl and let stand, covered with a plate or plastic wrap, to loosen the skins, at least 15 minutes. Peel the chiles, then slit them open and remove and discard the seeds, seed pod, and veins. Coarsely chop the chiles.

Cook the onion and garlic in the oil in a large, heavy skillet over medium heat until softened, about 3 minutes. Add the poblanos and the salt and cook, stirring, for 3 minutes. Transfer the mixture to a blender, add the chicken stock or broth and blend until smooth.

COOK THE CHICKEN

Put the chicken in a large bowl and toss with the salt.

Heat a large, heavy skillet over high heat until hot. Add the oil and swirl the pan to coat the bottom. Add the chicken and sauté, stirring, until the chicken is just cooked through, 3 to 5 minutes.

Stir the sauce into the chicken and heat through, about 3 minutes.

Make tacos with the accompaniments.

ACCOMPANIMENTS: *Warm corn tortillas, grated Monterey Jack cheese or Roasted Corn Salsa (p. 76)*

Roasted Corn Salsa

Roasting the corn gives it a deeper flavor that is complemented by the cumin that seasons this salsa.

MAKES ABOUT 2 CUPS

1 ear of corn, shucked

1 medium tomato, seeded and chopped

1 jalapeño or serrano chile, finely chopped

3 scallions, white and green parts, thinly sliced

2 tablespoons lime juice

½ teaspoon ground cumin

½ teaspoon salt

→ Bring an inch of water to a boil in a wide pot and add the corn. Cover and cook for 5 minutes. Remove from the water.

Heat a flat griddle or a grill until hot and roast the corn, turning on all sides, until many of the kernels are browned, 6 to 8 minutes total.

When the corn is cool enough to handle, cut the kernels from the cob and mix with the remaining ingredients in a bowl.

NOTE: *The salsa keeps chilled for 2 days.*

Sautéed Chicken with Guajillo-Avocado-Leaf Sauce

Pollo en salsa de chile guajillo y hoja de aguacate

MAKES 5 CUPS (15 TO 18 TACOS; SERVES 5 TO 6)

FOR THE SAUCE

2 ounces guajillo chiles, wiped clean, stemmed, seeded, and deveined

5 medium garlic cloves, unpeeled

Two ½-inch-thick slices of white onion

½ cup vegetable oil

1 (¼-ounce) package avocado leaves

1 teaspoon cumin seed

1 teaspoon salt

1 cup water

FOR THE CHICKEN

2 pounds boneless, skinless chicken breasts, cut into ½-inch cubes

1 teaspoon salt

3 tablespoons vegetable oil, divided

Traditionally chicken would be braised in this bright red guajillo sauce, infused with the lovely anise flavor of whole fresh avocado leaves. Unfortunately, fresh avocado leaves are hard to find in the U.S. (unless there is a tree near you), and packaged dried leaves are usually broken. To make up for that, fry the leaves to bring out their flavor and then blend them in the sauce.

PREPARE THE SAUCE

Heat a flat griddle or a large, heavy skillet over medium-low heat. Toast the chiles in batches, turning and pressing with tongs until they are fragrant, pliable, and have turned a brighter red, about 1 minute. Transfer the chiles to a bowl of cold water and let them soak to soften, about 20 minutes. Drain.

Toast the garlic and onion on the griddle or in a skillet over medium-low heat. Turn the garlic occasionally until it gives slightly when pressed (not completely softened), about 10 minutes. Cook the onion, turning once, until both sides are blackened and the onion is tender, about 20 minutes. Peel the garlic.

Heat the oil in a small, heavy skillet over medium-high heat until hot. Add the avocado leaves in two batches and fry until lightly browned, about 1 minute per batch. As they're fried, transfer the leaves to a blender.

Add the chiles, garlic, and onion to the blender along with the cumin seed, salt, and water and blend until smooth, at least 2 minutes.

COOK THE CHICKEN

Put the chicken in a large bowl and toss with the salt.

Heat a large, heavy skillet over high heat until hot. Add 2 tablespoons oil and swirl the pan to coat the bottom. Add the chicken and sauté, stirring, until the chicken is just cooked through, 3 to 5 minutes. Transfer the chicken to a clean bowl.

Fiery Arbol Chile Salsa

Salsa de chile de arbol

Keep this salsa on hand for those times when you want to add heat to a taco.

MAKES 1 CUP

½ pound tomatoes (2 small)

½ pound tomatillos (5 to 6), husked and rinsed

20 dried arbol chiles, stemmed

2 medium garlic cloves, peeled

½ teaspoon salt

→ Heat an oven or toaster oven to 500°F and line a baking pan with foil. Core the tomatoes and cut an X through the skin on the opposite end. Put the tomatoes, cored side up, and tomatillos on the tray and roast, turning the tomatillos over once halfway through, until the vegetables are browned and completely softened, 20 to 25 minutes for the tomatillos and about 30 minutes for the tomatoes.

Meanwhile, heat a flat griddle or a large, heavy skillet over low heat. Toast the chiles slowly, turning occasionally, until they are deep brown on all sides, about 8 minutes.

Put the tomatoes and tomatillos along with any juices from roasting into a blender with the chiles, garlic, and salt. Blend until smooth, at least 2 minutes, adding a little water if necessary to help blend.

NOTE: *This sauce keeps chilled for 1 week.*

Heat the remaining 1 tablespoon oil in the skillet over medium-high heat. Add the sauce and cook, stirring, until it thickens slightly, about 5 minutes. Stir in the chicken and any juices and stir over medium heat until heated through, 3 to 5 minutes, adding a little more water if necessary so the sauce coats the chicken.

Make tacos with the accompaniments.

NOTE: *This dish keeps chilled for 3 days.*

ACCOMPANIMENTS: *Warm corn tortillas, chopped onion, chopped cilantro, Fiery Arbol Chile Salsa (above) for heat, if desired*

Chicken "Flutes"

Flautas de pollo

**MAKES 4 *FLAUTAS*; SERVES
2 AS A SNACK OR A LIGHT
MEAL**

4 corn tortillas

1 cup shredded roasted or
Poached Chicken (p. 74)

Two 6-inch bamboo skewers

⅔ cup Cooked Tomatillo
Salsa (p. 33)

2 to 3 cups vegetable oil for
frying

¼ cup Mexican crema or
créme fraîche

⅓ cup crumbled queso fresco

Flautas get their name from their shape: a corn tortilla
rolled around a filling then deep-fried to hold its flutelike
shape. *Flautas* are considered fried tacos, or *tacos dorados*.
At one of Mexico City's most famous *flautas* stands they are
served leaning into a bowl with a thinned-down cooked tomatillo salsa that acts as soup and dipping sauce, sprinkled
with thick cream and queso fresco, and eaten by hand.

→ Place a tortilla on a plate, add ¼ cup of chicken, and roll the
tortilla around the filling, putting a plate on top of it once formed
to hold its shape. Continue with the other 3 tortillas and the rest
of the chicken. Once all of the *flautas* are rolled, pierce 2 together
with a bamboo skewer, forming a "raft." Do the same with the
remaining *flautas* and skewer.

Heat the tomatillo salsa, with a little chicken stock or water to
thin, if necessary, in a small saucepan and keep warm.

Heat the oil in a wok or a wide 4- to 5-quart pot over medium-
high heat until hot. Fry the 2 "rafts" in the oil, turning over once or
twice, until golden and crisp, 4 to 5 minutes. Transfer to a paper-
towel-lined plate to drain and remove the skewers, if desired.

Divide the tomatillo salsa between 2 wide, shallow bowls and
rest 2 *flautas* on the rim of each bowl with one end in the sauce.
Drizzle the *flautas* with crema or créme fraîche and sprinkle with
cheese. Hold the *flauta* with your fingers to eat, dipping the end
in the sauce.

Mole from Puebla

Mole poblano

**MAKES ABOUT 10 CUPS
SAUCE, OR 20 CUPS WITH
CHICKEN (ABOUT 60 TACOS;
SERVES 15 TO 20)**

One ½-inch-thick slice of
white onion

10 medium garlic cloves,
unpeeled

6 ounces dried mulato
chiles (12 large), wiped clean,
stemmed, slit open, and
deveined

4 ounces dried ancho
chiles (8 large), wiped clean,
stemmed, slit open, seeded,
and deveined

2 ounces dried pasilla
chiles (6 large), wiped clean,
stemmed, slit open, seeded,
and deveined

2 tortillas

½ cup plus 3 tablespoons
vegetable oil

½ ounce dried chipotle meco
chiles (2 to 3 tobacco-
colored), wiped clean,
stemmed, slit open, seeded,
and deveined

⅔ cup raw whole almonds

⅔ cup raw shelled peanuts

⅓ packed cup raisins

2 small ripe (mottled brown
or black) plantain, cut into
½-inch slices

⅔ cup unhulled sesame
seeds plus additional for
garnish

¼ teaspoon coriander seeds

continued on p. 84

This is considered Mexico's most complex sauce, a mas-
terpiece of nuanced flavors from chiles, nuts, fruit, seeds,
spices, and even a touch of chocolate. This rendition is from
Elvira Rueda, a marvelous cook from the city of Puebla and
the mother of my assistant, Rebecca Rosas. This recipe is
for a large quantity since the mole can be frozen, with or
without the chicken. If you are going to the trouble of making it, then have some friends over for a taco party or make
enough to keep for future meals. But if you prefer, cut the
recipe in half (but leave the amount of oil the same).

FOR THE TOASTED INGREDIENTS

→ Heat a comal, flat griddle, or heavy skillet over medium-low
heat, and toast the onion and garlic, turning occasionally, until
the garlic is just tender and golden brown with some blackened
spots, 8 to 10 minutes, and the onion is softened and charred on
both sides, about 20 minutes. Peel the garlic and set aside with
the onion.

While the garlic and onion are toasting, lightly toast the chiles
(except the chipotles) on the griddle a few at a time, turning and
pressing them down with tongs, until they are fragrant, 30 seconds to 1 minute per batch. Transfer the chiles to a large bowl of
cold water and let soak until softened, 20 to 30 minutes.

On another burner hold a tortilla with tongs directly over the
flame until it ignites, then transfer to a heatproof plate and let it
burn until completely blackened. Repeat with the other tortilla.

4 cloves

¼ teaspoon black peppercorns

¼ teaspoon allspice berries (5 large)

2 (3-inch) pieces Mexican cinnamon

¼ teaspoon aniseed

6 to 8 cups homemade chicken stock or canned broth

1½ teaspoons fine salt, or 1 tablespoon coarse salt

4½ ounces Mexican chocolate, such as Ibarra or Abuelita® (1½ tablets)

10 pounds poached or roasted chickens (about 3), or one 10-pound poached or roasted turkey, skinned and shredded

FOR THE FRIED INGREDIENTS

Have ready a medium bowl and a metal sieve set over a small heatproof bowl.

Heat ½ cup oil in a medium, heavy skillet over medium heat until it shimmers and fry the following ingredients in order one by one. Transfer them with a slotted spoon as they're fried to the medium bowl. (For ingredients that are difficult to scoop, empty the contents of the skillet into the sieve set over the small bowl to drain first, then return the oil to the skillet and place the fried ingredient into the medium bowl.)

Fry the chipotle chiles, turning frequently until they are puffed and very dark, about 3 minutes.

Fry the almonds, stirring, until they are golden, about 2 minutes.

Fry the peanuts, stirring, until they are golden, about 2 minutes.

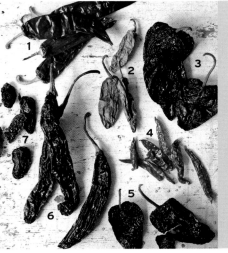

MEXICAN PANTRY

Dried Chiles

Dried chiles are a staple in Mexican cooking. The heat and flavor varies by type of chile. When choosing, look for whole pods (not broken) that are uniform in color. Most important, be sure to buy what the recipe calls for. Dried chiles can sometimes be mislabeled.

1. guajillo 2. chipotle meco 3. ancho 4. arbol 5. mulato 6. pasilla negra 7. chipotle morita

Fry the raisins, stirring, until they are puffed, about 1 minute.

Fry the plantain slices, turning over once, until golden, about 3 minutes.

Fry the unhulled sesame seeds and the whole spices in the oil remaining in the skillet until the seeds are golden, about 1 minute. Transfer everything, including the oil, to the medium bowl with the other ingredients.

Drain the toasted chiles in a sieve and purée them in a blender with the burnt tortillas and about 2 cups chicken stock or broth.

Heat the remaining 3 tablespoons oil in a wide, 7- to 8-quart, heavy pot over medium heat until hot, then add the chile purée and cook, stirring occasionally, until thickened slightly, about 10 minutes.

Meanwhile, working in 2 batches, blend the onion, garlic, and fried ingredients (from the medium bowl) along with 2 cups more chicken stock or broth per batch.

Add the mixture to the pot as it is puréed. Stir in the salt and chocolate, stirring until the chocolate is melted, then simmer, partially covered and stirring occasionally, for 45 minutes. Add more stock or broth as needed to maintain a velvety consistency (thick enough to coat a wooden spoon but not gloppy). Season to taste with more salt.

Add the chicken or turkey, reduce the heat to low, and cook until it is heated through, 3 to 5 minutes.

Make tacos with the accompaniments.

ACCOMPANIMENTS: *Warm corn tortillas, chopped white onion, toasted unhulled sesame seeds*

DRINK UP

Hibiscus Cooler

Agua de Jamaica

The floral and earthy flavor of dried hibiscus flowers may be familiar to you as one of the ingredients in Red Zinger® tea. Here I have only lightly sweetened the cooler. Add more sugar if you like, but the amount listed if reserving some for making the Hibiscus-Flavored Corn Tortillas on p. 16.

MAKES 1 QUART

5 cups water

2 ounces (1 heaping cup) dried hibiscus flowers (*flor de Jamaica*)

1/4 cup sugar or agave syrup

➔ Bring the water to a boil, then add the hibiscus flowers and the sugar or agave syrup and simmer for 5 minutes. Remove the pan from the heat and let the mixture cool to room temperature. Strain through a medium-mesh sieve into a pitcher, pressing on then discarding the flowers. Taste for sweetness and chill until cold. Serve over ice.

NOTE: *Hibiscus cooler keeps chilled for 1 week.*

Duck Legs Braised in Chipotle-Tomatillo Sauce

Pato en salsa de chipotle-tomatillo

MAKES 4 CUPS (12 TO 16 TACOS; SERVES 4 TO 5)

FOR THE SAUCE

1 ounce ancho chiles (2 large), wiped clean, stemmed, cut open, and seeded

½ pound tomatillos (5 or 6), husked and rinsed

½ cup chopped white onion

2 large garlic cloves, peeled

3 *chipotles en adobo*

1 tablespoon light brown sugar

1 teaspoon salt

½ teaspoon cumin seeds

5 peppercorns

2 allspice berries

1 cup water

FOR THE DUCK

3 pounds duck legs (4 to 6), skin and fat removed and reserved

½ teaspoon salt

1 tablespoon vegetable oil

1½ cups water

FOR THE DUCK CRACKLINGS

Skin and fat reserved from the duck legs

1 cup water

Because duck legs have so much fat, take off the skin before braising the legs, but don't throw it away! We'll make crispy duck *chicharrónes* with the skin to give crunch to the finished tacos.

MAKE THE SAUCE

➡ Heat a flat griddle or a large, heavy skillet over medium-low heat. Toast the ancho chiles, turning and pressing with tongs until they are fragrant, pliable, and have changed color slightly on the inside, about 1 minute. Transfer the chiles to a bowl of cold water and let them soak to soften, about 20 minutes. Drain.

Meanwhile, heat a toaster oven or oven to 500°F and line a baking pan with foil. Put the tomatillos on the pan and roast, turning the tomatillos over halfway through, until browned and completely softened, 20 to 25 minutes total.

Put the drained anchos and the tomatillos, including any juices from roasting, in a blender along with all the other sauce ingredients and blend until smooth, at least 2 minutes.

COOK THE DUCK

Heat the oven to 350°F.

Season the duck legs all over with the salt.

Heat a wide ovenproof casserole over medium-high heat until hot. Add the vegetable oil and swirl the pan so the oil coats the bottom. Add the duck legs (in batches if necessary) and brown on both sides, about 5 minutes total per batch. Transfer the duck legs to a plate and pour off and discard all but 1 tablespoon fat from the pan. Add the sauce and cook over medium heat, stirring, until thickened, 3 to 5 minutes. Stir in the water and bring to a boil. Return the duck legs to the sauce, turning to coat them with sauce. Cover the casserole and bake in the middle of the oven, turning the legs over halfway through to cook evenly, until the duck is tender, about 1½ hours.

Make the duck cracklings while the legs braise. Cut the reserved duck skin and fat into ½-inch-wide strips and put into a medium, heavy saucepan with the water. Bring to a boil and simmer over medium heat, stirring occasionally, until the water is evaporated and the skin fries to a golden brown in its own fat, 15–20 minutes.

Transfer the cracklings with a slotted spoon to a paper-towel-lined plate to drain.

FINISH THE TACOS

Remove the duck legs from the sauce and when cool enough to handle, shred the meat. Return the meat to the sauce and cook, stirring, until heated through, about 3 minutes.

Make tacos with the accompaniments and top with the duck cracklings.

ACCOMPANIMENTS: *Warm corn tortillas, chopped white onion, cilantro*

Pork

Brought by the Spanish conquest, the domesticated pig has become the most popular meat in Mexico. Not only was the meat adapted to the cooking methods of every region, but the fat from the pig also transformed those methods—pork lard was added to tamales and beans, and frying became a new way of cooking. Every part of the pig is used from the head to the tail; even the skin is fried and transformed into one of Mexico's most beloved specialties, *chicharrón*.

Several of the most prized tacos are made from pork. *Carnitas* (p. 114), from the central highlands, are made from pork that is stewed then crisp-fried in the fat left when the liquid evaporates, like a confit. *Tacos al pastor* (p. 110), thin slices of chile-marinated pork cooked on a vertical spit (an Old World method introduced by the Lebanese) that are topped with a pineapple and an onion to flick onto the taco, originated in Mexico City. *Cochinita pibil* (p. 103), the star in the Yucatecan crown, is pork

roasted in banana leaves (traditionally in a pit dug in the earth) with a fragrant annatto seed paste. You'll find these recipes in this chapter, all adapted for the home kitchen.

Other tacos included in this chapter fit in the category of *tacos de guisados*, or casserole dishes traditionally served with tortillas on the side, like the pork stewed in tomatillo sauce or pork stewed with a dried chile adobo.

Chorizo, spicy pork sausage, is used in many ways in Mexico. It is uncooked rather than cured like Spanish chorizo. If you can't find any in your area, make your own following the recipe I've provided—it's easy and there is no need for casings since the meat is removed from the casings for cooking anyway. I have paired it with pineapple or potato for delicious taco fillings. See the breakfast chapter for Scrambled Eggs with Chorizo Tacos (p. 144).

You'll also find some of my favorite salsa recipes to accompany these tacos. Vibrant Fresh Green Salsa (p. 115) is the perfect foil for *carnitas*; Creamy Green Salsa (p. 113)—creamy from the addition of avocado—is a great salsa to have on hand for almost any taco, and is a standard at my favorite *tacos al pastor* stand in Mexico City. The smoky Tomato-Chipotle Salsa (p. 130) is packed with flavor and lasts for at least a week. It's great to have on hand.

Be sure to make the Pickled Onions (p. 106), the classic accompaniment for *cochinita pibil*. They keep for at least a month, and you'll find yourself reaching for them to brighten up many tacos. If you make *tacos al pastor*, you'll be working with a whole pineapple, so I've included a recipe for *tepache*, a pineapple drink made with the pineapple rind, vinegar, and raw sugar. It is especially good with tequila and a touch of seltzer.

Tacos with Pork in Green Sauce

Tacos de cerdo en salsa verde

MAKES 5 CUPS (15 TO 20 TACOS; SERVES 6)

1½ pounds tomatillos (15 to 18), husked and rinsed

2 serrano or jalapeño chiles, stemmed

1 teaspoon cumin seed

3 allspice berries

1 whole clove

3 medium garlic cloves, peeled

½ cup coarsely chopped cilantro

1½ teaspoons salt, divided

3 pounds pork shoulder, cut into 1-inch pieces

2 tablespoons vegetable oil

The acidity of the tomatillos beautifully balances the fat of the pork shoulder, so when serving the tacos there is no need for lime wedges. The onion and additional cilantro provide crunch and fragrance.

In a 3-quart saucepan, cover the tomatillos and chiles with cold water and bring to a boil. Reduce the heat and simmer the vegetables uncovered, turning occasionally, until the tomatillos are tender and khaki-green all over but still intact, about 15 minutes. Reserve the cooking liquid.

Heat the cumin, allspice berries, and clove in a small, dry skillet over medium heat, shaking the pan or stirring the spices until they are fragrant and the cumin is a few shades darker, about 1 minute.

Put the spices in a blender along with 1 cup of the tomatillo cooking water and blend until the spices are ground. Using a slotted spoon, gently lift the tomatillos and chiles out of the remaining cooking water and put them in the blender along with the garlic, cilantro, and ½ teaspoon salt. Blend until smooth.

Pat the pork dry and season with the remaining 1 teaspoon salt. Heat the oil in a wide, heavy 4- to 5-quart pot over medium-high heat and brown the pork in batches without crowding, turning occasionally, about 8 minutes per batch.

Return all the meat to the pan and add the tomatillo sauce. Bring to a simmer, stirring to coat the meat, then reduce the heat. Simmer the pork, covered, stirring occasionally, until the meat is tender and the sauce is thickened, 1½ to 2 hours. If necessary, continue to cook uncovered to thicken the sauce. Shred the meat with two forks.

Make tacos with the accompaniments.

NOTE: *The pork in green sauce will keep chilled for 3 days.*

ACCOMPANIMENTS: *Warm corn tortillas, Mexican crema or sour cream, chopped white onion, chopped cilantro*

Chile-Braised Pork Tacos

Tacos de cerdo en adobo

MAKES 4 CUPS (15 TO 18 TACOS; SERVES 5 TO 6)

2 large ancho chiles (1 ounce), wiped clean, cut open, and seeded

4 large guajillo chiles (1 ounce), wiped clean, cut open, and seeded

1 teaspoon cumin seed

5 black peppercorns

1 clove

4 large garlic cloves, peeled

1½ cups water

2 tablespoons cider vinegar

¼ teaspoon dried oregano, preferably Mexican

1½ teaspoons salt, divided

2 pounds pork shoulder, cut into 1-inch pieces

2 tablespoons vegetable oil

An adobo is a versatile dried chile sauce and one of the easiest Mexican sauces to make. Here, pieces of pork are stewed in it, adding both an earthy, luscious flavor to the meat and balancing the richness of the pork with a slight acidity. A little avocado and chopped onion are all you need for a delicious taco.

→ Heat a flat griddle over medium-low heat. Toast the chiles in batches, turning and pressing with tongs until they are fragrant, pliable, and have turned a brighter red, about 1 minute over low heat. Transfer the chiles to a bowl of cold water and let them soak to soften, about 20 minutes. Drain.

Toast the cumin, peppercorns, and clove in a small, dry skillet over medium heat, stirring, until fragrant, about 1 minute.

Put the spices, drained chiles, garlic, water, vinegar, oregano, and ½ teaspoon salt in a blender and blend until smooth and the spices are completely ground, about 2 minutes.

Pat the pork dry and toss it with the remaining 1 teaspoon salt. Heat the oil in a 3- to 4-quart heavy pot over medium-high heat until it is hot, and brown the pork in batches, turning to brown each side, 6 to 8 minutes per batch. Transfer the browned pork to a bowl.

Return all the meat to the pan, then stir in the adobo from the blender until the meat is coated; cook for 1 to 2 minutes. Swish another ¼ cup water in the blender, add to the pot, and bring to a simmer. Cover the pot and simmer gently until the pork is tender and the sauce is thickened enough to coat it generously, about 1½ hours. Continue to cook uncovered, if necessary, to thicken the sauce. Shred the meat with two forks.

Make tacos with the accompaniments.

NOTE: *The chile-braised pork will keep chilled for 5 days.*

ACCOMPANIMENTS: *Warm corn tortillas, avocado slices and chopped white onion, or guacamole (p. 34).*

MEXICAN PANTRY

Mexican Oregano

Always used dried, Mexican oregano is slightly more pungent and less sweet than Greek oregano. It is available in little bags in Latino markets or online from Amazon.com.

Chorizo and Potato Tacos

Tacos de chorizo y papa

MAKES 4 CUPS (12 TO 15 TACOS; SERVES 4 TO 5)

1 pound boiling potatoes (about 2 large)

1 pound Mexican or Spanish chorizo

2 teaspoons dried oregano, preferably Mexican, crumbled

Salt

These are easy and satisfying tacos for any time of day, including breakfast. If you can't find Mexican chorizo, which is fresh not cured like Spanish chorizo, you can make your own following the recipe on p. 100. If you use Spanish chorizo, you'll need to finely chop it and sauté it in a little oil.

➞ Peel the potatoes and cut them into ½-inch dice. Cook in a saucepan of boiling salted water until they are just cooked through and still hold their shape, about 5 minutes. Drain.

Remove the casings from the chorizo and crumble (Mexican) or finely chop (Spanish) the meat. Cook the chorizo in a large skillet (add a teaspoon of oil if using Spanish chorizo) over medium heat, stirring, for 5 minutes. Add the potato and oregano and cook, stirring, for 5 minutes. Season with salt to taste.

Make tacos with the accompaniments.

ACCOMPANIMENTS: *Warm corn tortillas, guacamole (p. 34) or Fresh Tomato Salsa (p. 28)*

Homemade Mexican Chorizo

Depending on where you live, it may be easier to make your own chorizo than it will be to find it in the supermarket. Since Mexican chorizo is normally removed from its skin and used crumbled, there is no need to prepare and fill casings, so making your own chorizo is easy. Try to find dried guajillo chiles or guajillo chile powder, although using Mexican oregano will also help create the right flavor. Guajillo chiles have a bright earthy flavor that is not very spicy, so arbol chiles (or cayenne powder) are added for heat.

MAKES ABOUT 2¼ POUNDS CHORIZO

2 ounces dried guajillo chiles (8 large), wiped clean and stemmed, or 6 tablespoons guajillo (or New Mexican) chile powder

15 dried arbol chiles (⅓ ounce), stemmed and wiped clean, or 1½ teaspoons cayenne powder

4 large garlic cloves, peeled

2 teaspoons salt

2 pounds fatty ground pork (preferably from pork shoulder)

1½ tablespoons dried oregano, preferably Mexican

1 teaspoon ground cumin

½ teaspoon freshly ground black pepper

½ teaspoon ground allspice

¼ cup cider vinegar

➤ Slit open the guajillo chiles (if making your own powder) and remove (and reserve) the seeds. Heat a flat griddle or skillet over low heat and toast the guajillos slowly to dry them out, turning them and pressing down with tongs occasionally, until they are fragrant and the inner sides have turned a brighter red, about 5 minutes. Transfer the guajillos to a plate to cool.

Spread out the whole arbol chiles on the griddle (if making your own powder) and toast them, turning as they brown and blister on the outside, until quite dark, about 5 minutes. Transfer the arbol chiles to a plate to cool and open one to see if the seeds are also toasted—they should be a golden color. If not, add them to the griddle with the guajillo seeds and toast, stirring, until all the seeds are golden, about 2 minutes. Tear the cooled guajillo and arbol chiles into pieces, then grind with the seeds (in batches if necessary) in a coffee/spice grinder until finely ground.

Mince the garlic and mash it to a paste with the salt. Put the garlic mixture and the homemade chile powder (or the guajillo or New Mexican chile powder and cayenne) in a large bowl along with all the other ingredients and knead with your hands (wear protective gloves since the chiles can irritate skin) until well mixed. Cover the bowl with plastic wrap and let it chill for 2 to 24 hours to season.

NOTE: *The chorizo mixture will keep for 3 days in the refrigerator and also can be frozen for 3 months.*

Quick Chorizo and Pineapple Tacos

Tacos de chorizo y piña

MAKES 3 CUPS (10 TO 12 TACOS; SERVES 4)

1 cup chopped white onion

1 tablespoon vegetable oil or mild olive oil

1 pound Mexican or Spanish chorizo, preferably "hot"

1 teaspoon Mexican oregano (optional)

1 can (8 ounces) crushed pineapple

Salt

1 teaspoon cider vinegar (optional)

These supereasy tacos were created by my friend, Danny Flanigan from Watermill, New York. Whether you make them with Mexican chorizo or the easier-to-find Spanish chorizo that Danny uses (a great thing to have on hand since it is fully cooked and keeps for ages in the fridge), they are delicious. I like a final crunch of white onion, a spritz of lime, and a sprinkling of cilantro. Serve with avocado for a smooth finish.

Cook the onion in the oil in a large sauté pan over medium heat, stirring, for a few minutes until just softened.

Remove the casings from the chorizo and crumble (Mexican) or finely chop (Spanish) the meat. Cook the chorizo and oregano (if using), stirring, until heated through, if using Spanish chorizo, or if using Mexican chorizo, until cooked through, about 5 minutes. Add the crushed pineapple, including its juice or syrup, and stir for 1 minute more. Season with salt to taste and, if desired, add 1 teaspoon of cider vinegar for added acidity, especially if the pineapple comes in syrup.

Make tacos with the accompaniments.

NOTE: *If you have added vinegar to the mixture, you might not want to add lime wedges due to the additional acidity.*

ACCOMPANIMENTS: *Warm corn tortillas, avocado wedges, chopped white onion, chopped cilantro, lime wedges*

Yucatecan Pulled Pork Tacos

Cochinita pibil tacos

**MAKES 10 CUPS (30 TO
40 TACOS; SERVES 10 TO 12)**

1 teaspoon cumin seed

1 teaspoon black peppercorns

½ teaspoon allspice berries

1 dried arbol or other small
hot dried chile, stemmed, or
¼ teaspoon cayenne powder
(do not toast cayenne)

4 tablespoons annatto seeds
(achiote)

8 medium garlic cloves,
peeled

2 teaspoons salt

2 teaspoons dried oregano
(preferably Mexican),
crumbled

⅓ cup fresh orange juice

⅓ cup distilled white vinegar

1 large white onion, coarsely
chopped

6 pounds pork shoulder, cut
into 2-inch pieces

2 large frozen banana leaves,
thawed

½ cup water

This is a great recipe to make for a large party. The pork is deeply flavorful, redolent of earthy annatto seeds, aromatic spices, and the flavor from the banana leaves wrapped around the pork. In the Yucatán, a whole pig's worth of meat would be cooked in the ground, enough meat to feed a village. This dish lends itself to freezing, so it is perfect if you like to make large quantities of food on the weekends to freeze in portions for smaller meals during the week. Pickled onions (p. 106) are the classic accompaniment for *cochinita pibil tacos*—their acidity cuts the fat of the pork and provides spice.

PREPARE THE PORK

➥ Toast the cumin, peppercorns, allspice berries, and chile in a dry, heavy skillet over medium-low heat, stirring or shaking the pan until the spices are fragrant, 1 to 2 minutes. (If using cayenne powder, don't toast it.) Grind the toasted spices, and cayenne powder if using, with the annatto seeds to a powder in a coffee/spice grinder.

Mince the garlic and mash it to a paste with the salt.

In a large bowl stir together the ground spices, mashed garlic and salt, oregano, orange juice, and vinegar. Add the onion and pork and toss to season the meat evenly. Cover the bowl and marinate the pork, chilled, for at least 2 hours and up to 24 hours.

TOAST THE BANANA LEAVES

Turn a burner to medium high. Holding a banana leaf with your fingers, toast it by running it through the flame or over the burner, moving the leaf as it changes color to a brighter, shinier green (see the sidebar on p. 105). Toast the other side of the leaf.

Cut the toasted leaf in half. Line a large roasting pan with the banana leaf halves, leaving enough overhang on all sides of the pan to cover the pork once the pan is filled. If two pieces aren't enough, toast another banana leaf, then place in the pan. The leaves will bend more easily for wrapping if you cut off the coarse edge.

ROAST THE PORK

Heat the oven to 325°F.

Fill the lined roasting pan with the marinated pork, spreading it evenly, then drizzle the water on top. Fold the banana leaves over the pork, covering it completely, then cover the whole pan with foil. Bake the pork in the middle of the oven until it is very tender, 3 to 3½ hours.

To make the tacos, uncover the pork and shred it with two forks. Fill the tortillas with pulled pork and top with Pickled Onions and cilantro.

ACCOMPANIMENTS: *Warm corn tortillas, Pickled Onions (p. 106), chopped cilantro*

Toasting Banana Leaves

➡ Banana leaves are sold frozen in many supermarkets that offer Latino ingredients. They need to be defrosted for 1 to 2 hours before they can be toasted.

Toast a banana leaf directly in the flame of the burner on a gas stove. As you move it slowly though the flame you will see it change color to a brighter, shinier green. On an electric stove, toast a leaf by holding it over the burner until the color changes. Toast it again at the same speed on the other side and you are ready to use it as a flavorful wrapper for cooking (they are not for eating!). Leftover banana leaves can be refrozen for up to 1 month.

Pickled Onions

In the Yucatan you will find these bright pink pickled onions on every table. They pack a punch from the habanero chile.

MAKES 1½ CUPS

1 large red onion, halved lengthwise and thinly sliced lengthwise (3 cups)

1 habanero chile, very finely chopped

1 teaspoon dried oregano (preferably Mexican), crumbled

½ teaspoon salt

About 1 cup distilled white vinegar

➜ Bring a kettle of water to a boil and pour over the onion to cover in a heat-proof bowl. Let stand for 5 minutes to wilt, then drain.

Transfer the onion to a transparent container and stir in the chile, oregano, and salt. Add enough vinegar to just cover the onion and cool to room temperature. Chill, covered, until the onions turn bright pink, about 8 hours.

NOTE: *The pickled onions keep chilled for 1 month.*

Grilled Pork Tacos

Tacos de chuleta de cerdo

**MAKES 9 TO 12 TACOS;
SERVES 3 TO 4**

1 orange

1 lime

3 medium garlic cloves, peeled

1 teaspoon salt

½ teaspoon black peppercorns

Four ½-inch-thick bone-in pork chops (about 1½ pounds), or boneless pork chops, pounded to flatten

Vegetable oil for grill or griddle

Look for thin-cut (½-inch-thick) pork chops or buy boneless pork chops and pound them to ½ inch thick. The thin meat is penetrated quickly with a garlicky-citrusy marinade and is superfast to cook. I like the Roasted Tomatillo-Chipotle Salsa with the grilled pork, which adds acidity and smokiness, but you can substitute another salsa or guacamole.

Squeeze the juices from the orange and the lime into a blender and add the garlic, salt, and peppercorns. Blend until the pepper is ground. Pour the marinade into a wide container and put the pork chops in the marinade, turning them to season evenly. Cover and chill the chops in the marinade for at least 1 hour and up to 24 hours, turning occasionally.

Prepare a grill or heat a grill pan. Brush the grill rack or pan lightly with oil and cook the pork chops (in batches if necessary) until just cooked through, about 2 minutes a side. Transfer the chops to a plate to rest for a few minutes, then thinly slice the meat for tacos and mix with any juices on the plate.

Make tacos with the accompaniments.

ACCOMPANIMENTS: *Warm corn tortillas, Tomatillo-Chipotle Salsa (p. 109), avocado, chopped white onion, chopped cilantro*

Roasted Tomatillos

Roasting tomatillos deepens their flavor and creates a lovely slightly sweet syrup; this helps to balance their acidity. When boiled, their acidity comes out and is a welcome contrast to rich meats and cheeses.

Tomatillo-Chipotle Salsa

With the simple addition of some *chipotles en adobo*, this becomes a rich and smokey salsa.

MAKES 1 CUP

½ pound fresh tomatillos (5 or 6), husked and rinsed

3 large garlic cloves, peeled

2 tablespoons canned *chipotles en adobo*, including sauce

Rounded ¼ teaspoon salt

→ Heat an oven or toaster oven to 500°F and line a baking tray with foil. Put the tomatillos and garlic on the tray and roast for 10 minutes. Remove the garlic when it is browned and slightly softened. Turn over the tomatillos and roast for an additional 10 to 15 minutes until they are browned and softened all the way through.

Put the garlic and tomatillos into a blender with the chipotles and salt and blend until smooth. Cool to room temperature.

NOTE: *Because all the ingredients are cooked, this sauce will easily last for 1 week in the refrigerator.*

VARIATION

Tomato-Chipotle Salsa

→ Roast 2 medium tomatoes instead of the tomatillos in the same manner. Tomatoes may take up to 30 minutes total. Peel the tomatoes before adding them to the blender.

Chile-Marinated Pork Tacos with Roasted Pineapple

Tacos al pastor

MAKES 6 CUPS (20 TO 24 TACOS; SERVES 6 TO 8)

FOR THE MARINATED PORK

6 large guajillo chiles (1½ ounces), wiped clean, stemmed, seeded, and torn into large pieces

¾ cup water

1 cup chopped fresh pineapple (from a whole pineapple, see below)

½ cup white vinegar

2 teaspoons salt

4 medium garlic cloves

1 teaspoon dried oregano, preferably Mexican

½ teaspoon ground cumin

Pinch ground cloves

3 pounds thin boneless pork chops or thin slices of pork shoulder

FOR THE ROASTED ACCOMPANIMENTS

1 whole pineapple, peeled (reserve the rinds for the *tepache*, p. 112) and cut around the core into ½-inch-thick slices (chop enough of the pineapple for the marinade above)

1 large white onion, cut into ½-inch-thick slices

Oil

Traditionally the meat for these delicious tacos is marinated and layered on a vertical spit-roaster and cooked with a pineapple on top. This version provides the same amazing flavor but can be easily made at home on the stovetop or on a grill. Guajillo chiles give the marinade its bright red color.

MARINATE THE PORK

Put the guajillo chiles in a small saucepan with the water, chopped pineapple, vinegar, and salt, and bring to a boil. Simmer, uncovered, stirring occasionally, until the chiles are softened (they will turn a brighter red), about 10 minutes.

Put the chile mixture, including the liquid, into a blender along with the garlic, oregano, cumin, and ground cloves and blend until smooth, about 1 minute. Transfer to a wide bowl and cool to room temperature.

Flatten the pork between 2 sheets of plastic wrap with a meat pounder or heavy rolling pin (or have this done by the butcher) to ¼ inch thick. Dredge each piece in the chile mixture to coat both sides (add a touch more water if the mixture is too thick to coat easily) and layer in a plastic or glass container. Cover the container and chill for at least 6 hours and up to 24 hours.

ROAST THE ACCOMPANIMENTS

Heat the broiler and put a rack 5 to 6 inches below the heat (the second nearest level); alternatively, prepare a grill. Arrange the pineapple and the onion slices in one layer on a lightly oiled, large, four-sided baking sheet and brush the tops with oil. Broil, turning once, until the pineapple and the onion are browned and a little charred on both sides and cooked through, about 10 minutes for the onion and 15 to 20 minutes for the pineapple. Coarsely chop the pineapple and the onion and put them in a serving bowl.

COOK THE PORK

Heat a large grill pan or griddle, or prepare a grill, brushing the surface lightly with oil once it is hot. Cook or grill the meat in

batches until just cooked through, only about 1 minute per side. Transfer the meat to a platter as it is cooked, layering the pieces to keep them moist and collect the juices. Once all the meat is cooked, thinly slice the stack of meat and coarsely chop.

TO SERVE

Make tacos with the warm tortillas, filling them with small amounts of the meat followed by a little roasted pineapple and onion, then a small spoonful of one of the salsas and a sprinkling of cilantro.

ACCOMPANIMENTS: *Warm corn tortillas (preferably 4-inch), Creamy Green Salsa (p. 113) or Tomatillo-Chipotle Salsa (p. 109), chopped cilantro*

DRINK UP

Pineapple Drink

Tepache

MAKES ABOUT 1 QUART

Rind from 1 whole pineapple, cut into 1- to 2-inch pieces

1 quart (4 cups) water

½ cup cider vinegar; more as desired

4 ounces *piloncillo* (Mexican raw sugar) or ½ cup light brown sugar; more as desired

➡Put all the ingredients in a medium saucepan and bring to a boil. Simmer, uncovered, stirring occasionally to dissolve the sugar, for 20 minutes. Cool to room temperature. (If you have the time, chill the mixture in the fridge overnight to develop the flavor.)

Put the cooled mixture into a blender and blend until coarsely chopped to release more of the pineapple flavor. Strain through a fine-mesh sieve, pressing on the solids (discard any), and add more sugar or vinegar to balance the flavor if necessary. Chill until cold or serve over ice.

VARIATION

Tequila-*Tepache* Cocktail

➡Pour 2 ounces (¼ cup) of tequila over ice, then add 4 ounces (½ cup) *tepache*. Top off with seltzer.

Creamy Green Salsa

This is a thinnish creamy salsa typical in many Mexican taquerias. It is best made fiery hot (with both jalapeños) since a small amount has to stand up to all the other ingredients in a taco, but it will still have a kick if you use only one jalapeño.

MAKES 3 CUPS

½ pound fresh tomatillos (5 or 6), husked and rinsed

1 to 2 jalapeño chiles, stemmed

2 medium garlic cloves

1 teaspoon salt

⅓ cup chopped cilantro

Flesh from 1 avocado

⅔ cup water

→ Put the whole tomatillos and the jalapeños in a small saucepan with water to cover and bring to a boil. Lower the heat and simmer the vegetables, turning them occasionally so they cook evenly, until the tomatillos are khaki-green and tender without falling apart.

Transfer the tomatillos and one jalapeño to a blender and add the remaining ingredients. Blend until smooth. Add more water if necessary to make a pourable sauce. Taste for heat and add the other jalapeño, if desired (blend smooth again before serving).

NOTE: *Because of the avocado this sauce is best used the day it is made, though the acid from the tomatillos may keep it for another day in the refrigerator.*

Fried Pork Tacos

Tacos de carnitas

MAKES 6 CUPS (20 TO 24 TACOS; SERVES 6 TO 8)

3 pounds boneless pork shoulder, cut into 2-inch pieces

1½ teaspoons salt

¾ cup pork lard or vegetable oil

3 cups water

½ cup Coca-Cola or 2 tablespoons sweetened condensed milk

½ orange, cut into 2 wedges

1 medium white onion, cut into 1-inch wedges, layers separated

6 medium garlic cloves, peeled

2 teaspoons dried oregano, preferably Mexican

3 bay leaves

10 black peppercorns

Carnitas is one of the most beloved taco fillings in Mexico. The pork is cooked until it is fork-tender and the liquid has evaporated; then it is browned in the remaining fat. A little sugar—in this case Coca-Cola®—helps the browning and gives the meat a slightly sweet edge. The rich pork flavor is balanced by one of Mexico's "big guns" salsas made with raw tomatillos—Fresh Green Salsa, one of my favorites.

➥ Put the pork in a wide, heavy pot, then add the salt and toss. Add the remaining ingredients and bring to a boil (the liquid won't quite cover the meat). Cook the meat, uncovered, at a slow boil (about medium heat), stirring occasionally, until the meat is fork-tender and most of the liquid has evaporated (be careful not to let the meat start to burn because of the sugar in the cola), 1¼ to 1½ hours. Discard the orange pieces and the bay leaves.

Heat the oven to 450°F.

Transfer the *carnitas* to a medium roasting pan and roast, uncovered, in the oven until all the liquid has evaporated and the meat is browned, about 20 minutes. Shred the *carnitas* with two forks.

Make taco with the accompaniments.

ACCOMPANIMENTS: *Warm corn tortillas, Fresh Green Salsa (p. 115), chopped white onion*

MEXICAN PANTRY

Tomatillos

Tomatillos, or "little tomatoes" in Spanish are small, round fruits enclosed in a papery husk. They vary in size as well as color, from yellow to red and even purple. Tomatillos lend a tart, zesty flavor to salsas and sauces. Their husks need to be removed and they need to be rinsed before using.

Fresh Green Salsa

Because all the ingredients are raw, they have a lovely vibrant flavor that must be enjoyed the day it is made.

MAKES 1½ CUPS

½ pound tomatillos (5 to 6), husked, rinsed, and quartered

½ cup coarsely chopped cilantro

1 large scallion, white and green parts, coarsely chopped

1 fresh serrano or jalapeño chile, coarsely chopped

1 medium garlic clove

½ teaspoon salt; more as desired

Put all the ingredients in a blender and blend until finely chopped or smooth. Season to taste with additional salt.

Braised Chicharrón Tacos

Tacos sudados de chicharrón

**MAKES 12 TO 15 TACOS;
SERVES 4 TO 5**

FOR THE SAUCE

1 large tomato

1 white onion, sliced into
½-inch-thick rounds

1 jalapeño chile, stemmed

2 medium garlic cloves,
unpeeled

½ teaspoon salt

¼ teaspoon black pepper

1 tablespoon olive oil

FOR THE FILLING

4 ounces fried pig skin
(*chicharrón*), broken into
1-inch pieces

1 large tomato, seeded and
diced

½ medium white onion, diced

6 radishes, quartered and
thinly sliced

1 to 2 jalapeño chiles, finely
chopped

½ cup chopped cilantro

1 banana leaf

Try to find real fried pig skin (*chicharrón*) at your local Latino market; it makes these tacos extra delicious. I had these tacos at Sobrinos, Roberto Craig's restaurant in Mexico City; Roberto was kind enough to give me the recipe. The *chicharrón* is broken up and mixed with a tomato sauce and chopped vegetables to soften it, then steamed inside banana leaves until it is tender and succulent.

MAKE THE SAUCE

Heat a toaster oven or oven to 500°F and line a baking pan with foil. Core the tomato and cut an X through the skin on the opposite side. Put the tomato (cored side up), onion, jalapeño, and garlic cloves on the foil and roast the vegetables until they are browned and softened, 10 to 15 minutes for the jalapeño and garlic, 20 to 25 minutes for the onion, turning once, and 30 minutes for the tomato. Peel the garlic.

Add all the roasted vegetables to a blender along with the salt, pepper, and olive oil and blend until smooth.

MAKE THE FILLING

In a bowl stir together the sauce and the *chicharrón* and let stand for 15 minutes to start softening the *chicharrón*. Mix in the tomato, onion, radishes, jalapeño, and cilantro.

Holding the banana leaf with your fingers, toast it by running the leaf over a burner on medium high (see p. 105), moving the leaf over the burner as it changes color to a brighter, shinier green (it will be obvious when you try it). Toast the other side of the leaf.

Cut a piece of banana leaf to line a shallow steamer basket, leaving enough overhang to cover the filling. Put the filling on the banana leaf and wrap the leaf around it. Steam the filling for 20 minutes.

Make tacos with the accompaniments. If desired, the filling can be rolled up in the tortillas and served on a banana leaf.

ACCOMPANIMENTS: *Warm corn tortillas, guacamole (p. 34; optional)*

Meat

I owe my love and knowledge of adobo sauces to my good friend Roberto Santibañez, who wrote the book *Truly Mexican*. Adobo sauces are made from dried chiles (no nuts or seeds, like a mole) and very easy to make. They figure strongly in this chapter.

Start out by making the Adobo Marinade on p. 128. It is also used in other chapters, including for making Chile-Flavored Corn Tortillas (p. 15). Because it can be used for grilling all sorts of meat and seafood, think of it as a barbecue sauce. It lasts for at least 1 week and can be frozen. The Drunken Chile con Carne would be a great next step—it uses a whole recipe of the marinade and gets added flavor from a bottle of beer, tomato sauce, pickled jalapeños, and a touch of chocolate.

Grilling is a great cooking method for beef, especially when it's been marinated. The marinade in Grilled Garlic-Marinated Skirt Steak Tacos (p. 121) can be adapted to any steak. I chose skirt steak because it is one of the best steaks found in

Mexico; in fact, that is where I discovered it. The beef culture of the north, especially in the states of Chihuahua and Sonora, with their vast grazing plains, has developed greatly, and ranchers there have been producing increasingly good-quality meat. In the rest of the country, though, the steaks tend to be tougher, so they are best cut very thin. I've seen paper-thin slices of rib eye seared in a matter of seconds at Tizoncito's in Mexico City, served in a taco with a *costra*, or crust of melted cheese; and *cecina*, long thin sheets of beef that have been salted, are found everywhere in Mexico.

Goat and lamb are also popular in Mexican dishes. While beef is best from the northern plains, sheep thrive on the central plateau and goats on the more rugged lands of eastern states like Coahuila and Nuevo Leon and mountainous regions throughout the country.

Grilled Garlic-Marinated Skirt Steak Tacos

Tacos de arrachera a la parilla con ajo

MAKES 18 TO 24 TACOS; SERVES 6

3 pounds skirt steak (about 3 long steaks)

3 tablespoons finely chopped garlic

3 tablespoons olive oil

Coarse salt, to taste

3 tablespoons fresh lime juice, or to taste

Skirt steak, a toothsome and very flavorful cut of beef that is a favorite of mine, is excellent for grilling or pan-searing.

➤ If necessary, trim membrane from the steaks by pulling it away in one piece. Place the steaks in a baking dish, rub with the garlic and oil, and let marinate, chilled, for at least 30 minutes and up to 1 day.

Prepare a grill or heat a broiler.

Season the steaks generously with coarse salt and grill them over glowing coals or direct heat on a gas grill for about 3 minutes on each side for medium-rare. (Alternatively, broil the steaks 3 inches from the heat for about 4 minutes on each side.) Transfer the steaks to a platter and drizzle with lime juice.

Let the steaks stand, loosely covered with foil, for 5 minutes. Cut them diagonally across the grain into thin slices.

Make tacos with the accompaniments.

ACCOMPANIMENTS: *Warm corn or flour tortillas, Charred Spring Onions (p. 122), Fiery Arbol Chile Salsa (p. 79) or Tomatillo-Chipotle Salsa (p. 109)*

MEXICAN PANTRY

White and Green Onions

White, not yellow, onions are common in Mexican markets. They have less sugar than yellow onions, so they tend to keep better when they are cut, and they have a refreshing crunch when raw. Green onions have a bulb base and are larger than scallions. They can be found in farmers' markets in spring and early summer and in Latino markets the rest of the year.

Charred Spring Onions

Cebollitas asadas

Farmers' markets in the spring and throughout the summer abound with spring onions. Bigger than scallions, they have round white bulbs about 1 inch in diameter and long greens similar to scallions. When roasted on a grill or griddle until charred, they make a great accompaniment to steak and steak tacos.

MAKES 20

20 spring onions or large scallions (about 4 bunches)

1 tablespoon vegetable oil or mild olive oil

½ teaspoon salt

1 lime, halved

Prepare a grill or heat a broiler.

Trim the roots and ends from the spring onions, leaving about 8 inches of green stalk

In a large bowl toss the onions with the oil and salt.

Grill the onions on the grill, turning them with tongs 3 or 4 times, for 5 to 7 minutes or until softened and lightly charred. If you don't have a grill, broil the onions on a broiler pan about 3 inches from the heat, turning them with tongs 2 or 3 times, for 10 to 12 minutes.

Transfer the onions to a platter and squeeze the lime halves over them.

Sautéed Skirt Steak with Spicy Tomato Sauce

Arrachera con jitomate

MAKES 15 TO 20 TACOS; SERVES 5 TO 6

2 pounds skirt steak (about 2 long steaks)

1½ teaspoons salt, divided; more as needed

2 tablespoons vegetable oil, divided

1 medium white onion, thinly sliced

1 (28-ounce) can diced tomatoes

2 or 3 fresh serrano or jalapeño chiles, coarsely chopped, including seeds

This humble, comforting dish gets a real kick from the roasted serrano chile sauce.

Cut the steaks crosswise into 2 or 3 pieces each that will fit in a large skillet. Pat each steak dry with paper towels and season with 1 teaspoon salt.

Heat a dry, heavy 12-inch skillet over medium-high heat until hot and add 1 tablespoon oil. Sauté the steaks in batches, adding the remaining tablespoon of oil to the second batch. Cook for about 3 minutes on each side for medium-rare, and transfer to a platter to rest for 5 minutes while making the sauce.

Add the onion to the skillet and cook over medium heat until slightly softened, about 3 minutes. Add the tomatoes (including the juice), chiles, and the remaining ½ teaspoon salt and simmer, uncovered, stirring occasionally, until the sauce is thickened slightly and the onion is crisp-tender, about 5 minutes. Season with more salt to taste.

Thinly slice the steaks diagonally across the grain and stir into the sauce along with any juices that have accumulated on the platter; warm through.

Make tacos with the accompaniments.

ACCOMPANIMENTS: *Warm corn or flour tortillas, Serrano Chile Salsa (p. 125; optional)*

Serrano Chile Salsa

Salsa torreada

This sauce was given to me by Obdulia Trejo of Guanajuato, who works as a cook in Mexico City. It is blended with the oil the chiles were cooked in, giving it a creamy texture, like mayonnaise. Its fiery heat will give a lift to any taco.

MAKES ABOUT ⅔ CUP SAUCE

¼ pound fresh serrano chiles (about 12), stemmed

½ cup vegetable oil

¼ medium white onion, halved

2 large garlic cloves, peeled

1 tablespoon water

½ teaspoon salt

Cut a slit through the skin of each chile from tip to tail. Heat the oil in a small skillet over medium-high heat until hot. Add the chiles along with the onion and garlic and fry, stirring and turning the chiles over, until they are browned and blistered all over, about 5 minutes. Transfer the chiles, onion, and garlic with a slotted spoon to a plate and cool until cool enough to handle, 5 minutes. Reserve the oil from the skillet. Peel the chiles using a paring knife and transfer them to a blender along with the onion, garlic, water, salt, and the oil in the skillet. Blend until smooth.

Note: *The salsa keeps chilled for 3 days.*

Drunken Chile con Carne Tacos

Tacos de chile con carne

**MAKES 4 CUPS (12 TO
16 TACOS; SERVES 4 TO 5)**

2 pounds beef chuck cut into
1-inch pieces

1 teaspoon salt; more to taste

3 tablespoons vegetable oil;
more as needed

1 cup chopped white onion

1 recipe Adobo Marinade
(p. 128)

1 (8-ounce) can tomato sauce

1 (12-ounce) bottle beer

1 cup water

1 (7-ounce) can pickled jalapeño chiles with juice, chiles
sliced

1 ounce Mexican or bitter-
sweet chocolate

This chile con carne is made with chunks of beef, much more
common in Mexico than ground beef. It is slowly braised with
beer and chocolate for full flavor.

Season the beef with the salt. Heat the oil in a 5- to 6-quart
heavy pot over medium-high heat and brown the meat in batches,
without crowding, turning occasionally, 6 to 8 minutes per batch;
transfer the meat to a bowl as it is browned.

Sauté the onion in the fat remaining in the pot (or add an extra
tablespoon) over medium heat until softened, about 3 minutes.
Add the Adobo Marinade and cook, stirring, for 5 minutes to
thicken slightly. Stir in the tomato sauce, beer, water, and pickled
jalapeños and juice and bring to a boil. Return the beef to the pot
and simmer, covered, until tender, 1½ to 2 hours.

Stir in the chocolate until melted and season with salt to
taste. If necessary, simmer uncovered until the sauce is just thick
enough to coat the meat.

Make tacos with the accompaniments.

NOTE: *Chile con carne will keep chilled for 3 days.*

ACCOMPANIMENTS: *Warm corn tortillas, chopped white onion,
chopped cilantro*

Adobo Marinade

MAKES 1½ CUPS

5 large garlic cloves,
4 unpeeled and 1 peeled

4 large ancho chiles
(2 ounces), wiped clean,
cut open, and seeded

½ teaspoon cumin seed

5 peppercorns

1 clove

½ cup water

1 teaspoon cider vinegar

¼ teaspoon dried oregano,
preferably Mexican

½ teaspoon salt

½ teaspoon sugar

This is a very versatile sauce. It can be used as a marinade for grilled meats, chicken, and seafood, or as a sauce for braising meats or making chile. Made with ancho chiles, it is full-bodied, earthy, and slightly sweet. When made with guajillo chiles (see the variation below), it is slightly brighter in color and flavor.

⇢ Heat a flat griddle or large, heavy skillet and toast the unpeeled garlic cloves, turning once or twice until they are slightly softened (they'll give slightly when squeezed) and browned in patches, about 8 minutes total. Peel.

Meanwhile, in the same griddle or skillet, toast the chiles in batches, turning and pressing with tongs until they are fragrant, pliable, and have turned a brighter red, about 1 minute. Transfer the chiles to a bowl of cold water and let them soak to soften, about 20 minutes. Drain.

Toast the cumin, peppercorns, and clove in a small skillet over medium heat, stirring, until fragrant, about 1 minute.

Put the spices, drained chiles, toasted garlic and raw garlic clove, water, vinegar, oregano, salt, and sugar in a blender and blend until smooth, about 2 minutes, adding more water, 1 tablespoon at a time, only if necessary to help the mixture blend properly.

NOTE: *The Adobo Marinade keeps chilled for 1 week or frozen for 1 month.*

VARIATION

⇢ Substitute 2 ounces guajillo chiles (about 8 large) for the ancho chiles for a brighter red yet equally delicious sauce without the sweet edge from the anchos.

Ground Beef Chili Tacos

MAKES 4 CUPS (12 TO 16 TACOS; SERVES 4 TO 5)

1 cup chopped onion

3 garlic cloves, minced

2 tablespoons vegetable oil

1 tablespoon ground cumin

1½ teaspoons salt

2 pounds ground beef chuck

1 recipe Adobo Marinade (made with ancho chiles; p. 128)

Just about everyone in the U.S. has grown up eating some type of ground beef chili. This version uses a Mexican dried chile sauce, or adobo, as its base and also includes the extra hit of cumin more common in American versions. Refried beans (pp. 27–28) would make a great addition to these tacos; spread them on the tortillas before adding the chili.

Cook the onion and garlic in the oil in a wide, medium pot over medium heat until softened, about 3 minutes. Add the cumin and salt and cook, stirring, for 1 minute. Add the meat and cook, stirring, over medium-high heat until the meat is no longer pink, then add the Adobo Marinade and bring to a simmer. Simmer the chile, partially covered, for 30 minutes.

Make tacos with the accompaniments.

ACCOMPANIMENTS: *Warm corn or flour tortillas, chopped onion, grated Cheddar cheese*

Tacos with Shredded Meat in Tomato-Chipotle Sauce

Tacos de tinga de carne

MAKES 5 CUPS (15 TO 20 TACOS; SERVES 5 TO 6)

FOR THE MEAT

1 pound flank steak or brisket, cut into 2-inch pieces

1 pound lean pork shoulder, cut into 2-inch pieces

3 quarts water

1 teaspoon salt

Peelings and ends from two large white onions (see sauce)

6 large garlic cloves, unpeeled

FOR THE SAUCE

2 large onions, peeled and tops and bottoms trimmed, then thinly sliced lengthwise

3 tablespoons vegetable oil

1½ teaspoons salt, divided; more to taste

1½ teaspoons brown sugar

2 pounds tomatoes, quartered

2 chipotle chiles from a can of *chipotles en adobo*

1 cup water

6 bay leaves

FOR THE TORTILLAS

Corn tortillas

About ¼ cup vegetable oil

Simple or Spicy Refried Beans (pp. 27-28)

Guacamole (p. 34)

David Ortega, a chef and caterer in Mexico City, gives cooking classes to a series of regular devotees. I joined his class the night he was making these delicious tacos. David doesn't like to waste anything so he used the ends and skins of the onion to flavor the cooking liquid, then turned the cooking liquid into a delicious consommé. Brushing the tortillas with a little oil (they should not end up greasy but softer) helps them absorb the sauce from the meat without breaking.

COOK THE MEAT

Put the meat in a large pot with the water and salt and bring to a simmer, skimming off the fat as it rises to the surface.

Meanwhile, heat a dry, flat griddle or large, heavy skillet and toast the peelings and ends of the onions and the unpeeled garlic cloves until everything is blackened in patches and the garlic is slightly softened, about 8 minutes. Transfer the vegetables (with peelings) to the pot with the meat. Simmer, partially covered, until the meat is fork-tender, 2½ to 3 hours. (Alternatively, cook the meat in a pressure cooker for 45 minutes.)

MAKE THE SAUCE WHILE THE MEAT IS COOKING

Cook the onion in the oil in a wide, heavy pot over medium-high heat with ½ teaspoon salt and the sugar, stirring, until golden brown and blackened in spots, 10 to 15 minutes.

Blend the tomatoes, chipotle chiles, water, and remaining 1 teaspoon salt in a blender until smooth. Strain through a medium-mesh sieve into the pot with the onion, discard any solids left in the strainer, and boil the sauce until it has thickened to a velvety texture and is a deep red color, 30 to 45 minutes.

SHRED THE MEAT AND FINISH THE DISH

When the meat is tender, transfer the pieces to a cutting board and finely shred the meat using two forks.

Add the meat to the sauce along with the bay leaves and enough broth from the pot to moisten the meat, 1 to 2 cups. Simmer the meat in the sauce, partially covered, for 30 minutes. Uncover the meat and season with more salt to taste. Continue to simmer, if necessary, until the sauce is thick enough to coat the meat. Remove the bay leaves.

MAKE THE TACOS

Heat a flat griddle or large, heavy skillet over medium-low heat until hot. Lightly brush one side of the tortillas with oil, stacking them as oiled (which will lightly oil the second side). Heat the tortillas, a few at a time depending on the size of your pan, and turning them as they soften, until hot, 1 to 2 minutes total; stack on a plate as heated. Spread a spoonful of refried beans on a tortilla, then top with some of the meat and guacamole. Serve the Fiery Serrano-Lime Salsa on the side. Continue to make tacos in the same manner.

NOTE: *The* tinga *will keep chilled for 5 days or frozen for 1 month.*

ACCOMPANIMENTS: *Fiery Serrano-Lime Salsa (p. 133)*

Fiery Serrano-Lime Salsa

Salsa de chile serrano con limón

This is chef Ortega's favorite spicy serrano salsa. He serves it to spice up his tacos with Shredded Meat in Tomato-Chipotle Sauce.

MAKES ABOUT ²/₃ CUP

6 fresh serrano chiles, stemmed

¹/₃ cup lime juice

1 teaspoon salt, or to taste

➡ Heat a dry, flat griddle or a large, heavy skillet over medium heat until hot and roast the chiles, turning them as they brown and blister until they are tender, about 8 minutes. Put them in a tightly sealed plastic bag for 15 minutes to help loosen the skins. Peel the chiles with a paring knife.

Put the chiles in a blender with the lime juice and salt and blend until smooth. Season with more salt to taste to balance the acidity of the lime juice.

NOTE: *The salsa keeps chilled for 3 days.*

Pan-Seared Sweetbreads

Mollejas a la plancha

**MAKES 9 TO 12 TACOS;
SERVES 3 TO 4**

1 pound sweetbreads

1½ teaspoons salt, divided

1 tablespoon vegetable or mild olive oil

I am a sweetbread lover and this is one of my favorite ways to eat them—crisp on the outside and creamy on the inside. You will probably have to order them in advance from your butcher.

Soak the sweetbreads in a large bowl of cold water and chill for about 8 hours to remove any blood, changing the water occasionally.

Drain the sweetbreads, then put them in a medium saucepan and fill with water to cover by 1 inch. Add 1 teaspoon salt and bring just to a boil. Immediately reduce the heat and simmer the sweetbreads, uncovered, until firm, 3 to 5 minutes. Drain them in a colander and transfer to a bowl of cold water to stop the cooking.

Using a small paring knife, cut away any fat and pull away as much membrane and connective tissue as possible without breaking up the sweetbreads.

Slice the sweetbreads on the diagonal into ½-inch-thick slices and season lightly with the remaining ½ teaspoon salt.

Heat a flat griddle over medium-high heat until hot. Brush the griddle with some of the oil and sear the sweetbreads, in batches if necessary, on both sides, until browned, about 1 minute per side.

Make tacos with the accompaniments.

ACCOMPANIMENTS: *Warm corn or flour tortillas, Creamy Green Salsa (p. 113) and Charred Spring Onions (p. 122), or Fresh Tomato Salsa (p. 28)*

Seared Shoulder Lamb Chops with Pasilla-Tomato Sauce

Chuletas de cordero con salsa de chile pasilla

MAKES 15 TO 18 TACOS; SERVES 5 TO 6

FOR THE SAUCE

2 ounces pasilla negra chiles (6 chiles), wiped clean, stemmed, cut open, and seeded

1 pound tomatoes (3 medium)

2 large garlic cloves, peeled

1 teaspoon oregano, preferably Mexican

1 teaspoon cumin seed

1 bay leaf

1 teaspoon salt

1½ cups water, divided

2 tablespoons vegetable oil

FOR THE LAMB

3 pounds lamb shoulder chops, about ¾ inch thick

1 teaspoon salt

1 or 2 tablespoons vegetable oil

The deep flavor of pasilla chiles goes well with lamb. In warm weather, the chops can be brushed with the oil and grilled.

MAKE THE SAUCE

Heat a dry, flat griddle over medium-low heat until hot and toast the chiles in batches, turning and pressing with tongs until they are fragrant, pliable, and have changed color slightly inside, about 1 minute. Transfer the chiles to a bowl of cold water and let them soak to soften, about 20 minutes. Drain.

Meanwhile, heat a toaster oven or oven to 500°F and line a baking pan with foil. Core the tomatoes and cut an X through the skin on the opposite end. Put the tomatoes, cored side up, on the foil and bake until the tomatoes are blackened and softened, about 30 minutes.

Combine the chiles and the tomatoes in a blender with the garlic, oregano, cumin seed, bay leaf, salt, and 1 cup water and blend until smooth (the bay leaf should be completely pulverized), about 3 minutes, adding more water, if necessary, to blend.

Heat the oil in a deep 4-quart pot over medium heat until warm, then add the sauce and cook, stirring, for 5 minutes. Add the remaining ½ cup water and simmer gently, partially covered and stirring occasionally, until thickened, about 20 minutes. Check the seasoning for salt.

COOK THE LAMB

Pat the lamb dry with paper towels and season with the salt.

Heat 1 tablespoon of the oil in a large skillet and sear the lamb in batches, without crowding, until browned but still pink inside, 2 to 3 minutes per side. Transfer the chops as cooked to a cutting board.

Cut the lamb in slices around the bone and make tacos with the sauce and the accompaniments.

NOTE: *The sauce keeps covered and chilled for 5 days.*

ACCOMPANIMENTS: *Warm corn tortillas, chopped white onion, lime*

Lamb Braised in Guajillo Sauce

Cordero al horno

**MAKES 18 TO 21 TACOS;
SERVES 6 TO 7**

1½ ounces guajillo (or New Mexican) chiles (6 large), wiped clean, stemmed, cut open, seeded, and deveined

1½ tablespoons annatto seeds

2 teaspoons cumin seed

3 large garlic cloves, peeled

¼ cup distilled white vinegar

2½ teaspoons salt, divided

¾ cup water

3 pounds boneless lamb shoulder (or 4 pounds with bone), cut into 2-inch pieces

4 bay leaves

The acidity of the guajillo sauce balances the richness of the lamb in this recipe adapted from Estela Salas Silva, a cooking teacher from Tlaxcala, Mexico.

Heat a dry, flat griddle over medium heat until hot. Toast the chiles in batches, turning and pressing down with tongs, about 1 minute per batch. Put the chiles in a bowl with cold water to soak for 30 minutes. Drain.

Toast the annatto seeds and the cumin seed in a dry, small, heavy skillet over medium heat, stirring, until fragrant and a shade darker. Cool on a plate, then transfer to a coffee/spice grinder and grind to a powder.

Heat the oven to 350°F.

Put the soaked chiles in a blender along with the powdered seeds, the garlic, vinegar, 1½ teaspoons salt, and the water and blend until smooth (add a little more water if necessary to blend).

Season the lamb with the remaining 1 teaspoon salt and put in a 3-quart baking dish with the sauce and the bay leaves, stirring to combine.

Bake, covered with foil, until the lamb is fork-tender, about 2½ hours.

Make tacos with the accompaniments.

NOTE: *The lamb can be marinated in the sauce before baking for up to 8 hours. The braised lamb will keep chilled for 3 days.*

ACCOMPANIMENTS: *Warm corn tortillas, avocado slices and chopped white onion, or guacamole (p. 34)*

Goat Braised in Guajillo Sauce

➡ Substitute goat for the lamb.

Beef Short Ribs Braised in Guajillo Sauce

➡ Substitute 4 pounds short ribs on the bone or 3 pounds boneless short ribs for the lamb.

MEXICAN PANTRY

Annatto Seeds

Annatto seeds (*achiote*) are brick red-colored and taste of the earth. They are an important flavoring in Yucatecan foods. They can be found in the spice section of supermarkets carrying Latin-American products or ordered online from Amazon.com.

Breakfast

If you ask a Mexican for a breakfast taco he will look at you funny because he won't know what you mean. That is because Mexicans will eat any taco anytime of the day. Americans, on the other hand, think egg dishes are for breakfast. Eggs typically aren't served as a taco but rather are served accompanied by tortillas to eat the eggs with. It amounts to the same thing and is the reason that anything ends up being a taco filling.

In this chapter you'll find typical egg dishes made taco-friendly so they can be picked up and eaten out of hand. The exception is the traditional *huevos embodegados,* or "warehoused eggs," which I couldn't resist including since I love the novelty of putting a raw egg inside a tortilla and having it cook as the tortilla puffs. For a full experience, eat "warehoused eggs" with the bed of beans they're served on. The breakfast burrito, the ultimate pick-up breakfast, is more of an American invention, but delicious nevertheless.

If you'd like to have a Mexican brunch, make a couple of different kinds of scrambled eggs and have the tortillas warm in a basket. Serve a couple of salsas on the side, some cooked or refried beans, and guacamole or sliced avocadoes in a bowl. Be sure to make a fruit cooler and perhaps Mexican hot chocolate or the hot fruit drink called *atole.* Before serving the eggs, offer some fresh papaya with lime wedges.

Mexican Scrambled Egg Tacos

Tacos de huevos revueltos a la Mexicana

**MAKES 4 TO 6 TACOS;
SERVES 2 TO 3**

½ cup chopped white onion

2 tablespoons vegetable oil

1 cup chopped, seeded
tomato (1 medium)

1 chopped serrano or jalapeño
chile (remove the seeds for
less heat)

6 large eggs

2 tablespoons milk or
Mexican crema

½ teaspoon salt

These are the quintessential scrambled eggs in Mexico,
practically a *pico de gallo* cooked with the eggs. Like all
Mexican breakfasts, the presence of chile makes this a good
dish for the morning after a late night. Try this breakfast
with a fruit cooler (see p. 143).

Cook the onion in the oil in a medium nonstick skillet over
medium heat, stirring, for 1 minute. Add the tomato and chile and
cook, stirring, for 2 minutes more.

Whisk the eggs with the milk or crema and the salt, then add to
the pan and cook, stirring, until just set, about 2 minutes.

Make tacos with the accompaniments.

ACCOMPANIMENTS: *Warm corn or flour tortillas, sliced avocado,
chopped cilantro*

DRINK UP

Fruit Coolers

Aguas frescas

Replace your canned juices and sodas with these fruit coolers, which are really easy to make. I have been on a crusade to introduce them whenever I have a chance. The strength can vary from rich and juicy for breakfast to more thinned down with water, which is more traditional, for the rest of the day, hence the name in Spanish, which translates to "fruit water." These drinks are also a great way to use up leftover cut fruit.

MAKES ABOUT 5 CUPS

2 to 3 cups cut-up fruit such as melon, watermelon, mango, papaya, pineapple, grapes, cactus fruit, or strawberries

2 cups water; more as desired

1 to 2 cups ice

1 to 2 tablespoons mint leaves (optional; good with strawberries and pineapple)

Sugar

Juice of 1 lime

➜ Put the fruit, water, ice, and mint (if desired) in a blender and blend until smooth (you don't want chips of ice). Taste and add sugar or lime juice as desired and blend again. If your fruit has seeds (strawberries or watermelon), strain through a medium-mesh sieve. Serve in a pitcher with more ice. Thin with more water for a very light drink if desired.

NOTE: *To get the most out of one lime, peel it with a knife, including all the white pith, then cut it in half lengthwise and cut out the inner pith. Put the peeled lime in the blender with the fruit.*

VARIATIONS

➜ Substitute basil for the mint.

➜ Add a banana to make a breakfast smoothie.

➜ For a very minty drink, add a whole handful of mint leaves.

Scrambled Eggs with Chorizo Tacos

Tacos de huevos revueltos con chorizo

MAKES 9 TACOS; SERVES 3

½ pound Mexican chorizo, casings removed and meat finely chopped if not crumbly

1 tablespoon vegetable oil

½ cup chopped white onion

8 large eggs

2 tablespoons Mexican crema or milk

Salt

This is a totally satisfying breakfast. Be sure to make a refreshing melon or pineapple *agua fresca* (see the sidebar on p. 143) to quench your thirst.

Cook the chorizo with the oil in a medium nonstick skillet over medium heat, stirring, until it starts to give off its oil. Add the onion and cook, stirring, until the onion is softened and the chorizo is cooked, about 5 minutes.

Whisk the eggs with the crema or milk, then add to the pan and cook, stirring, until just set, about 2 minutes. Season with salt to taste, if necessary.

Make tacos with the accompaniments.

NOTE: *If you've made your own chorizo (see p. 100) or are using Spanish chorizo, you will need to add 2 tablespoons of oil to the skillet when cooking the chorizo.*

ACCOMPANIMENTS: *Warm corn tortillas, Roasted Tomato-Serrano Salsa (p. 145; optional), sliced avocado, chopped cilantro*

Roasted Tomato-Serrano Salsa

Salsa de molcajete

This thin salsa gets its texture from being mashed in a stone mortar. Although you can make this salsa in a blender, the blender will "whiten" the tomato. Another alternative is to work the tomato through a medium-mesh sieve and finely chop the serranos.

MAKES ABOUT ¾ CUP

2 medium tomatoes

4 serrano chiles, stemmed

1 teaspoon coarse salt or ½ teaspoon fine salt

➡ Heat a toaster oven or oven to 500°F and line a baking pan with foil. Core the tomatoes and cut an X through the skin on the opposite end. Put the tomatoes, cored side up, and the chiles on the foil and bake, turning the chiles occasionally, until the chiles are browned and softened, about 15 minutes, and the tomatoes are blackened and softened, about 30 minutes.

Put the chiles in a zip-top plastic bag and let them sweat for 10 to 15 minutes to loosen their skins. Remove the skins using a paring knife. Peel the tomatoes.

Put the chiles and the salt (using coarse salt will help grind the chiles) in the mortar and use a pestle to grind to a paste. Add the peeled tomatoes and their juices and mash. Check the seasoning for salt, and add more if needed.

NOTE: *The salsa will keep chilled for 5 days.*

Breakfast Burrito

SERVES 4

Four 10- to 12-inch flour tortillas

4 tablespoons vegetable oil, divided

1 cup chopped white onion

1 large tomato, chopped

2 chipotle chiles from a can of *chipotles en adobo*, chopped, including some sauce

2 cups Cooked Beans in Broth (p. 148), without liquid, or 2 (15-ounce) cans pinto or black beans, rinsed and drained

¾ teaspoon salt, divided

8 large eggs

2 tablespoons Mexican crema or milk

1 cup grated Monterey Jack cheese

1 ripe avocado, peeled, pitted, quartered, and sliced

½ cup chopped cilantro

Burritos come from the north of Mexico, where flour tortillas are king. These make a complete breakfast in a package. They can be wrapped in foil to keep them warm.

Heat the oven to 350°F.

Wrap the flour tortillas together flat in foil and heat in the oven until warm, 10 minutes.

While the tortillas are heating, heat 2 tablespoons of the oil in a large, heavy skillet over medium heat and cook the onion, stirring, until golden, about 10 minutes. Add the tomato, chipotles, beans, and ½ teaspoon salt and cook, stirring until heated through, for about 5 minutes.

In a medium nonstick skillet, heat the remaining 2 tablespoons oil over medium heat. Scramble the eggs and crema or milk with a fork and add them to the pan. Cook the eggs, stirring, until curds form, season with the remaining ¼ teaspoon salt, and remove from the heat when they're still slightly moist.

Lay a warm tortilla flat and arrange the fillings on it in a row side by side: ¼ of the eggs, ¼ of the bean mixture, ¼ of the cheese, ¼ of the sliced avocado, and ¼ of the chopped cilantro. Fold up the bottom of the tortilla over some of the filling and fold in the sides to make an open package. Repeat with the remaining tortillas and serve the burritos immediately.

VARIATION

Rice and Beans Burrito

Substitute 2 cups of warm cooked rice for the eggs.

Cooked Beans in Broth

Frijoles de olla

MAKES 8 TO 9 CUPS

1 pound dried pinto or black beans

12 cups water

½ cup chopped white onion

3 medium garlic cloves, peeled

2 sprigs epazote or 2 bay leaves

1 teaspoon salt

Pinto beans are more common in central and northern Mexico, while black beans are used in Veracruz and elsewhere on the east coast of Mexico.

Put the beans and the water in a large pot with the onion, garlic, and epazote or bay leaves and bring to a boil. Lower the heat and simmer, partially covered, until the beans are tender, 1¾ to 2 hours. Add the salt and simmer for a few minutes more.

NOTE: *The beans will keep chilled (cool completely first) for 1 week or frozen for 3 months.*

Fried Eggs Ranchero Style

Huevos rancheros

**MAKES 4 TACOS;
SERVES 2 TO 4**

4 corn tortillas

About 3 tablespoons vegetable oil, divided

About ½ cup Simple or Spicy Refried Beans (pp. 27-28)

4 large eggs

In this classic Mexican breakfast, the refried beans are normally served alongside a taco. Here, though, they form part of the taco. If you pick these up to eat with your fingers, instead of eating them with a fork and knife, make sure to put a plate underneath for any spillage!

⟶ Heat the oven to 200°F.

Heat a flat griddle over medium heat until hot. Brush the tortillas very lightly with some of the oil on both sides, stacking them as oiled. Heat the tortillas one by one on both sides on the griddle until hot but still soft, about 30 seconds a side, and transfer to a baking sheet in one layer. Spread a rounded tablespoon of refried beans on each one, leaving a border, and put them in the oven to warm the beans.

Heat the remaining oil (about 2 tablespoons) in a large nonstick skillet over medium heat until hot. Break the eggs in the pan and fry until the bottoms are golden, about 3 minutes. Carefully turn the eggs over and cook for 1 minute more, just to seal, but not cook, the yolks. Turn over and place each one on top of the refried beans on a tortilla. Spoon a little salsa over the egg and serve.

ACCOMPANIMENTS: *Roasted Tomato-Serrano Salsa (p. 145), Cooked Tomatillo Salsa (p. 33), or Tomatillo-Chipotle Salsa (p. 109)*

Hard-Cooked Eggs and Pumpkin Seed Sauce Tacos

Tacos al estilo de papadzules

MAKES ABOUT 3 CUPS; 6 FULL TACOS; SERVES 3

FOR THE FILLING

½ cup hulled green pumpkin seeds

3 peppercorns

2 allspice berries

1 clove

1 cup chicken broth or water

¼ teaspoon salt

1 tablespoon vegetable oil

6 hard-boiled eggs, coarsely chopped

FOR THE TORTILLAS

¼ cup vegetable oil

6 corn tortillas

Papadzules are a breakfast specialty of the Yucatán, where tortillas are dunked in a simple pumpkin seed sauce and then filled with hard-cooked eggs and rolled up like enchiladas. This recipe mixes the pumpkin seed sauce with the eggs as a filling for tacos, with spicy tomato-habanero salsa on top.

Put the pumpkin seeds and the whole spices in a medium, dry heavy skillet and cook over medium heat, stirring, until most of the pumpkin seeds are plumped and rounder (you will hear popping), without browning, 3 to 5 minutes.

Transfer the mixture to a blender and blend with the chicken broth or water and the salt.

Heat the oil in a small, heavy saucepan over medium-low heat and add the pumpkin seed sauce, stirring until heated through. Add the chopped hard-boiled eggs and cook, without boiling, until just heated through.

Heat the oven to 200°F.

Heat a flat griddle over medium heat until hot. Brush the tortillas very lightly with some of the oil on both sides, stacking them as oiled. Heat the tortillas one by one on both sides on the griddle until hot but still soft, about 30 seconds a side, and transfer to a baking sheet in one layer; keep warm in the oven as they are heated. Put about ½ cup of filling on each tortilla, then a spoonful of Yucatecan Tomato-Habanero Salsa and a scattering of pickled onions. Fold 2 tortillas side by side on plates.

ACCOMPANIMENTS: *Yucatecan Tomato-Habanero Salsa (p. 151), Pickled Onions (p. 106)*

Yucatecan Tomato-Habanero Salsa

Salsa de jitomate con habanero

Like the *salsa de molcajete* (p. 145), this is a thin roasted-tomato-based sauce. This one features the searing heat of a habanero, the classic chile of the Yucatán. This salsa is great for eggs and is the usual accompaniment for *papadzules*. Try it also on the Tacos with Shredded Chicken and Onion (p. 73).

MAKES 1 CUP

1 pound tomatoes (3 medium)
1 habanero chile, stemmed
½ teaspoon salt

→ Heat a toaster oven or oven to 500°F and line a baking pan with foil. Core the tomatoes and cut an X through the skin on the opposite end. Put the tomatoes, cored side up, on the foil and bake until they are blackened and softened, about 30 minutes.

Put the tomatoes, the habanero, and the salt in a blender and blend, leaving some texture.

Note: Yucatecan Tomato-Habanero Salsa will keep chilled for 1 week.

Allspice Berries

For many Americans, allspice is a familiar powdered spice used in apple pies. The whole dried allspice berry *(pimienta gorda* or *pimienta de Jamaica)*, which is available in the spice section of most supermarkets, is twice or three times the size of a peppercorn. The complex flavor has hints of other spices like cinnamon and clove, which is how it got the name "allspice."

"Warehoused" Eggs

Huevos embodegados

MAKES 4 EGGS;
SERVES 2 TO 4

About 6 ounces corn tortilla dough (p. 17)

4 large eggs

Salt

The cook for Mexican artist Carmen (Ricky) Parra, who lives on the Pacific coast near Zihautanejo, makes this dish for breakfast. To make it, you have to first make tortillas from raw tortilla dough. When the tortillas puff, take them off the fire, slit them open, and plop a raw egg inside (hence the name). Then reseal the partially cooked tortilla and put it back on the fire to finish cooking along with the egg.

Heat a large, flat griddle over medium heat until hot, about 2 minutes.

Pinch off 1½ ounces of dough to make a 1½-inch ball, then press in a tortilla press between two rounds of plastic to yield a 6-inch tortilla.

Peel off 1 plastic round, then, holding the tortilla over the edge of your palm, carefully peel off the other round so the tortilla is dangling from your palm. Transfer the tortilla to the griddle by letting the dangling edge touch it and slowly pulling your hand back as you lay the tortilla down on the griddle. This will take a little practice, but it is better than flipping a tortilla onto the griddle, because it rarely ends up lying flat.

Cook until the edges lift just slightly from the griddle, about 15 seconds. Turn over (you can lift the edge of the tortilla with a butter knife or spatula to help you but then grab it with your fingers and flip it over). Cook until a few faint brown spots appear on the underside, about 45 seconds. Turn over again and cook until the tortilla inflates (pressing on the edges of the tortilla with your fingers will help it inflate; if the tortilla doesn't inflate it won't work for this dish so finish cooking it—45 seconds—and move on to the next one). Remove the inflated tortilla from the heat with a spatula

(it will not be fully cooked). Use the point of a sharp knife to slit the edge of the pocket large enough to drop in an egg.

Crack an egg in a cup then, holding the tortilla open with one hand, pour the egg in with the other hand along with a small sprinkling of salt, and seal the tortilla with a little water on your fingers as best you can; return to the griddle. Repeat with the remaining tortillas.

Cook the filled tortillas, turning them over once, until the whites are cooked, 3½ to 4 minutes.

To serve, put some whole beans on each plate and put the egg-filled tortillas on top. Drizzle with one of the salsas and sprinkle with the cheese.

ACCOMPANIMENTS: *Warm Cooked Beans in Broth (p. 148), Tomatillo-Chipotle Salsa (p. 109) or Cooked Tomatillo Salsa (p. 33), crumbled queso fresco*

MEXICAN PANTRY

Mexican Cinnamon

Mexican cinnamon *(canela)*, also called Ceylon cinnamon, is a soft, thin bark cinnamon that originated from Ceylon. Its flavor is subtler and more floral than the hot cinnamon Americans are accustomed to. It is worth seeking out in Latino markets; if you don't have one near you, order from gourmetsleuth.com.

Atole

An atole (from the Nahuatl atolli) is a hot drink thickened with tortilla flour or masa. Whether you make a fruit atole (usually made with pineapple, strawberries, or guava) or a chocolate atole—called a *champurrado*—it is a great addition to a Mexican breakfast.

Fruit Atole

MAKES ABOUT 6 CUPS

5 cups water, divided

1½ cups chopped fruit (pineapple, strawberries, or guava)

½ cup sugar; more to taste

½ cup corn tortilla flour (masa harina), such as Maseca®

➜ Bring 2 cups of water to a boil in a medium, heavy saucepan.

Meanwhile, put the fruit in a blender with the sugar, tortilla flour, and the remaining 3 cups of water and blend until smooth, at least 1 minute to blend the fruit completely.

Pour the mixture through a medium-mesh sieve into the boiling water. Bring the mixture back to a boil, stirring, then reduce the heat and simmer gently, stirring occasionally, for 15 minutes. Add more sugar to taste, if necessary.

Chocolate Atole

Champurrado

MAKES ABOUT 5 CUPS

5 cups water

½ cup corn tortilla flour (masa harina), such as Maseca

¼ cup sugar

1 stick Mexican cinnamon

One 3-ounce tablet Mexican chocolate, such as Abuelita® or Ibarra, broken into sections

➜ Put the water in a medium, heavy saucepan and whisk in the corn tortilla flour. Add the sugar and the cinnamon and bring to a boil, whisking constantly. Add the chocolate, whisking to melt, and simmer, stirring, for 15 minutes. Remove and discard the cinnamon.

Quesadillas,
Sopes, and Tostadas

There are so many ways to use tortilla masa or tortillas that the subject could fill a book of its own. So while it might seem odd to include this chapter in a book on tacos, there are a number of these Mexican favorites that you can pick up like a taco, and in this chapter you'll find some of the most common. (Enchiladas and tortillas that are bathed in sauce and eaten with a knife and fork are not included here.)

The distinctions between all of these types of Mexican fare might seem small, but they make a difference in the kinds of fillings that can be used. Quesadillas are traditionally made with raw dough, filled, and then fried (the word "quesadillas" indicates the presence of cheese, but the form has evolved beyond the use of just cheese). Any filling that is dry enough not to moisten the tortilla is good to use. A *sope* is a slightly thick corn tortilla that has an edge on it to hold the filling. In addition

to the recipes in this chapter, try *sopes* with the Yucatecan Pulled Pork Tacos (p. 103) or the Duck Legs Braised in Chipotle-Tomatillo Sauce (p. 87). Tostadas, toasted or fried tortillas, can be piled with different meat or seafood mixtures. A layer of refried beans (or mashed avocado) will help hold everything together, some shredded lettuce will freshen the taste, and a little cream and cheese will add the finishing touch.

The quesadillas, *sopes*, and tostadas I've included use fillings that are also perfect in tacos. I have given recipes for small and large versions to be served as hors d'oeuvres or as a main course. If you're having a taco party, look to these recipes to round out your menu.

Chorizo and Potato Crescents

Chorizo and potato quesadillitas

MAKES ABOUT 36

1 large boiling potato (about ½ pound), peeled and cut into ¼-inch dice

½ pound chorizo, preferably Mexican, casing removed and meat finely chopped, if necessary

1 tablespoon vegetable oil plus 3 to 4 cups for deep-frying

1 teaspoon dried oregano (preferably Mexican), crumbled

¼ teaspoon salt, or to taste

1 recipe Corn Tortilla dough (p. 9)

These mini-quesadillas make a great hors d'oeuvre and can be served with guacamole or just about any salsa for dipping —I like Fresh Green Salsa (p. 115). Use your imagination to vary the filling.

In a saucepan of boiling salted water cook the potato until it is just cooked through, about 3 minutes. Drain in a colander.

Cook the chorizo with the oil in a medium, heavy skillet over moderate heat, stirring to break up the meat, for 5 minutes. Add the potato, oregano, and salt and cook, stirring, for 5 minutes. Transfer the filling to a bowl to cool completely.

Pinch off a ½-ounce piece of dough to make a ¾-inch (marble-size) ball. Put in a tortilla press lined with two 5-inch rounds of thin plastic and press into a 3½- to 4-inch round.

Remove the top piece of plastic and put a teaspoon of filling on the round of dough. Using the bottom piece of plastic as a support, lift the edges of the dough over the filling to enclose and press the edges together with your fingers to seal (see Making Mini-Quesadillas on p. 161).

Remove the plastic and transfer the crescent to a plastic-lined baking pan. Cover with another sheet of plastic wrap so the dough doesn't try out. Make more crescents in the same manner, reusing the plastic rounds and keeping the crescents covered with plastic wrap.

Heat the remaining oil in a wok or a 4-quart heavy pot until a deep-fat thermometer registers 375°F. Fry the crescents in batches of 8 to 10 until golden, 2 to 3 minutes, transferring them with a slotted spoon to a paper-towel-lined plate to drain and making sure the oil returns to 375°F between batches.

Serve the warm crescents with the salsa.

NOTE: *Formed crescents can be kept chilled, covered tightly with plastic wrap, for up to 6 hours before frying.*

ACCOMPANIMENT: *Fresh Green Salsa (p. 115)*

Making Mini-Quesadillas

Put a teaspoon of filling in the center of the dough.

Holding onto the plastic, lift the edges of the dough over the filling.

Pinch the sides of the mini-quesadilla together with your fingers, using the plastic as support.

Cheese Quesadillas

Quesadillas de queso

MAKES 8 TO 12; SERVES 4

8 to 12 homemade or store-bought corn tortillas

½ pound shredded Oaxaca or Monterey Jack cheese (2 cups)

6 pickled jalapeño chiles, chopped

12 squash blossoms, petals torn, or epazote leaves (optional)

In Mexico, a true quesadilla is made with raw corn tortilla dough and either cooked dry on a comal (flat griddle) or fried (see the mini-quesadillas on p. 161). I find it hard to cook the raw dough through on the comal though, so I used fully cooked tortillas. These are cheese-filled quesadillas but you could use any other filling—mushrooms (p. 36) or chard and potato (p. 29) are two other classics. Add some cheese to hold the sides of the quesadillas together as they bake.

Heat a dry, flat griddle over medium heat until hot, at least 2 minutes.

Put a few (depending on the size of your griddle) tortillas on the griddle at the same time and while they heat, mound ¼ cup of cheese in the middle of each and top with a sprinkle of jalapeños and some torn squash blossoms or one or two epazote leaves, if using. Fold each tortilla over the filling to create a half-moon. Continue to cook on one side then flip the tortilla over to cook the other side until the cheese is melted and the tortilla is just golden, about 2 minutes total.

Make more quesadillas in the same manner, serving them as they are made or keeping them warm in a 200°F oven.

ACCOMPANIMENT: *Fresh Green Salsa (p. 115) or Roasted Tomato-Serrano Salsa (p. 145)*

Bean and Goat Cheese *Sopes*

Sopes de frijol y queso de cabra

**MAKES ABOUT 18 SMALL
SOPES; SERVES 6 AS AN HORS
D'OEUVRE OR FIRST COURSE**

½ recipe Black-Bean-
Flavored Corn Tortilla dough
(p. 14) or regular Corn Tortilla
dough (p. 9)

2 tablespoons vegetable oil

1 recipe Spicy or Simple
Refried Beans (pp. 27-28)

8 ounces goat cheese, sliced
or crumbled

¾ cup chopped red onion

½ cup chopped cilantro

These *sopes* are inspired by some I ate at La Ciruela, a restaurant in the lovely town of Tepoztlán, which is just outside
of Mexico City and surrounded by majestic mountains. They
are a satisfying appetizer that could be followed by any one
of the seafood tacos in this book.

➡ Heat a dry, flat griddle over medium heat until hot, at least
2 minutes. Heat the oven to 350°F.

Pinch off a ½-ounce piece of dough to make a ¾-inch (marble-
size) ball of dough. Press lightly in a tortilla press between two
pieces of plastic to make a slightly thick 3-inch round.

Remove the plastic and transfer the tortilla to the griddle. Cook
until the edges just start to lift, about 30 seconds, then turn the
tortilla over. Cook the second side for 45 seconds and turn over
again. Cook for another 45 seconds, then remove from the heat.
(Since the tortillas are thicker than usual they will not yet be completely cooked.)

Using your thumb, "drag" some of the slightly raw dough toward the edge of the tortilla and pinch it against your forefinger to
create a "wall" all the way around the tortilla. (The tortilla will be
hot so wear a protective glove if desired.)

Return the *sope* to the griddle and cook for another 30 seconds
on each side. Transfer to a cloth-lined tortilla basket to keep warm
while making more *sopes* in the same manner.

Arrange the *sopes* in one layer on a baking pan. Drizzle a little
oil (about ¼ teaspoon) on each *sope*, then spread with a tablespoon of refried beans and top with about a tablespoon of the goat
cheese.

Warm the *sopes* in the oven for 8 minutes and serve sprinkled
with the onion and cilantro.

Making *Sopes*

Drag some of the slightly raw dough toward the edge of the tortilla with your thumb and pinch it against your forefinger to create a wall around the tortilla.

Chicken *Sopes*

Sopes de pollo

**MAKES 12 LARGE *SOPES*;
SERVES 4 AS A FIRST COURSE
OR LIGHT MEAL**

1 recipe Corn Tortilla dough
(p. 9)

2 tablespoons vegetable oil

¾ cup Cooked Tomatillo
Salsa (p. 33)

2 cups shredded chicken
(from 1 rotisserie or poached
chicken; see p. 74)

¾ cup chopped white onion

½ cup Mexican crema or sour
cream, thinned slightly with
water for drizzling

½ cup crumbled queso fresco

Chopped cilantro (optional)

If you don't want to make these from scratch, use store-bought tortillas and make them Puebla-style, without sides. Just cut the tortillas down to 4-inch rounds with a cookie cutter so they are manageable to pick up, and go light on the toppings.

Heat a dry, flat griddle over medium heat until hot, at least 2 minutes. Heat the oven to 350°F.

Pinch off a 1¼-ounce piece of dough to make a scant 1½-inch ball of dough. Press lightly in a tortilla press between two pieces of plastic to make a slightly thick 4-inch round.

Remove the plastic and transfer the tortilla to the griddle. Cook until the edges just start to lift, about 15 to 30 seconds, then turn the tortilla over. Cook the second side for 45 seconds and turn over again. Cook for another 45 seconds, then remove from the heat. (Since the tortillas are thicker than usual they will not yet be completely cooked.)

Using your thumb, "drag" some of the slightly raw dough toward the edge of the tortilla and pinch it against your forefinger to create a "wall" all the way around the tortilla. (The tortilla will be hot so wear a protective glove if desired.)

Return the *sope* to the griddle and cook for another 30 seconds on each side. (If using store-bought tortillas, put them on the griddle to warm.) Transfer to a cloth-lined tortilla basket to keep warm while making more *sopes* in the same manner.

Arrange the *sopes* in one layer on a baking sheet. Drizzle a little oil (about ½ teaspoon) on each *sope*, then a scant tablespoon salsa. Top with a little shredded chicken and finish with a little onion, cream, and cheese. Warm the *sopes* in the oven for 5 minutes and serve sprinkled with cilantro, if desired.

Chicken Tostadas

Tostadas de pollo

**MAKES 6 TOSTADAS;
SERVES 6**

4 cups shredded chicken
(from 1 rotisserie or poached
chicken; see p. 74)

2 cups Fresh Tomato Salsa
(p. 28)

3 cups shredded iceberg
lettuce

6 large radishes, halved and
sliced

1 recipe Simple or Spicy
Refried Beans (pp. 27-28)

½ cup vegetable oil

6 corn tortillas

1 avocado, halved, pitted, and
peeled

½ cup Mexican crema or sour
cream

¼ cup crumbled queso añejo
(aged white cheese, also
called *cotija*) or ricotta salata

Tostadas are fried or baked tortillas mounded with a fresh salady shredded meat topping, and one is enough for a whole meal. These can be eaten out of hand, but beware that they're messy, so you might want to use a knife and fork instead. Although the base—also called a tostada—can be bought, I prefer to fry my own.

➡ In a large bowl stir together the chicken, salsa, lettuce, and radishes.

In a small saucepan, heat the refried beans to warm.

Heat the oil in a medium, heavy skillet over medium-high heat until hot. Cook the tortillas one at a time, turning once or twice, until golden and crisp, about 1 minute each. Transfer the tortillas to a paper towels to drain then transfer each to a plate. (Alternatively, bake the tortillas whole following the directions for tortilla chips on p. 23.)

Spread the tortillas thickly with the refried beans, then top with a mound of the chicken mixture. Top with a slice or two of avocado, drizzle with cream, and sprinkle with cheese.

Crab Hors d'Oeuvre Tostadas

Tostaditas de jaiba

**MAKES 24 TOSTADAS; SERVES
6 TO 8 AS AN HORS D'OEUVRE**

1 pound jumbo lump
crabmeat, shredded
and picked over

1 cup Fresh Tomato Salsa
(p. 28), with the ingredients
very finely chopped, drained
of any liquid

6 to 8 corn tortillas

½ cup vegetable oil

2 avocadoes

½ teaspoon salt

These small bites of crab salad are easily put together and
a great way to start a meal. Follow them with Grilled Garlic-
Marinated Skirt Steak Tacos (p. 121) or Duck Legs Braised in
Chipotle Tomatilla Salsa (p. 87).

Stir together the crabmeat and salsa.

Cut 2-inch rounds out of the tortillas with a cookie cutter (3 or
4 per tortilla).

Heat the oil in a medium, heavy skillet over medium-high heat
until hot. Cook the tortilla rounds a few at a time, turning once or
twice, until golden and crisp, about 1 minute per batch. Transfer
the rounds to a paper-towel-lined plate to drain.

Mash the avocado with the salt. Spread a little of the avocado
on each *tostadita*, then mound with some of the crab mixture.

MEXICAN PANTRY

Avocado Leaves

Avocado leaves (*Hojas de Aguacate*) have a wonderful aniselike
flavor and can be used fresh or dried. Dried avocado leaves look
like large (4 to 6 inches long) bay leaves and can be found in
Latino supermarkets or ordered online from gourmetsleuth.com.

Metric Equivalents

liquid/dry measures

U.S.	Metric
¼ teaspoon	1.25 milliliters
½ teaspoon	2.5 milliliters
1 teaspoon	5 milliliters
1 tablespoon (3 teaspoons)	15 milliliters
1 fluid ounce (2 tablespoons)	30 milliliters
¼ cup	60 milliliters
⅓ cup	80 milliliters
½ cup	120 milliliters
1 cup	240 milliliters
1 pint (2 cups)	480 milliliters
1 quart (4 cups; 32 ounces)	960 milliliters
1 gallon (4 quarts)	3.84 liters
1 ounce (by weight)	28 grams
1 pound	454 grams
2.2 pounds	1 kilogram

oven temperatures

°F	Gas Mark	°C
250	½	120
275	1	140
300	2	150
325	3	165
350	4	180
375	5	190
400	6	200
425	7	220
450	8	230
475	9	240
500	10	260
550	Broil	290

Index